The Lost Mission was shortlisted for
Gordon Graham Prize for Naga Literature 2021

A TRUE STORY OF
LOVE, SACRIFICE & BETRAYAL

THE LOST MISSION

PEKINGTO Y. JIMO

THE LOST MISSION
Copyright © 2020 by PekingtoY. Jimo
ISBN 978-1-8382191-1-6

All rights reserved.
No part of this publication may be reproduced, stored in a retrieval system, or transmitted in any form or by any means, electronic, mechanical, photocopying or otherwise, without prior written consent of the publisher except as provided by under United Kingdom copyright law. Short extracts may be used for review purposes with credits given.

Main translation in use: NKJV

Scripture quotations marked NKJV are taken from the New King James Version®. Copyright © 1982 by Thomas Nelson. Used by permission. All rights reserved.

Emphasis within Scripture quotations is the author's own.

Published by
Maurice Wylie Media
Your Inspirational Christian Publisher

DISCLAIMER
This book is intended neither as an attempt to bring into hatred or contempt, nor to incite or excite disaffection towards either the Government of India or any of the Naga National Political Groups. This is but an honest attempt to give an account of 312 Naga Army, who for the love of their people, went through an excruciating mission to China, but were betrayed, rejected, and left forgotten for over half a century.

For more information visit
www.MauriceWylieMedia.com

DEDICATED TO THE SOLDIERS
WHO LOST THEIR LIVES
AND TO THOSE WHO RETURNED HOME

Contents

		Page
Certification from the veterans		7
Acknowledgements		15
Preface		17

Chapters

1	The Road to China	21
2	The First Battle	38
3	Strangers in a Brother's Land	45
4	Crossing the Border	52
5	China rolls out the Red Carpet	63
6	A Bridge too Far	83
7	Who will make it home?	89
8	The Enemy Awaits	105
9	Courage in the Face of Adversity	110
10	Hunger – The Enemy Within	117
11	Death and Casualties Surrounded Us	124
12	Please don't leave me behind	129
13	Do not Shoot! I Surrender!	133
14	Almost Home	138
15	The March of Betrayal	145
16	Your Reward Awaits	153
	The Lost Mission (Poem)	174
	Postscript	177
	The Veterans' Photos	179

Appendix

I	The Command Enrolment	193
II	Heroes Fallen in the Mission	203
III	Heroes detained for life in Indian Prisons	207
IV	Copy of Detention Order	211

Certification from the veterans

We, the undersigned Naga Army veterans, who undertook the dreadful Diplomatic Mission to China during the year 1967-69, hereby acknowledge the facts recorded in the book, *'The Lost Mission'* written by Mr. Pekingto Y. Jimo.

We further certify that the historical facts and information contained in the book are true and genuine as they have been narrated and contributed to the author by us as per our personal participation and experiences in the Mission.

1. Captain Sanguto Chase
4th Battalion, 2nd Brigade
1st Division, Southern Command
Naga Army

2. Captain Sakole Yokha
5th Battalion, 2nd Brigade
1st Division, Southern Command
Naga Army

[signature]

3. Lieutenant Dr. Samson Luikham,
7th Battalion, 3rd Brigade
1st Division, Southern Command.
Naga Army

[signature, dated 21/11/2018]

4. 2nd Lieutenant Rowndar Anal,
7th Battalion, 3rd Brigade
1st Division, Southern Command.
Naga Army.

[signature]

5. 2nd Lieutenant Yekhalu Jimo
Naga Army No. 1832, 14th Battalion,
5th Brigade, 2nd Division
Central Command, Naga Army.

[signature]

6. 2nd Lieutenant K. Zhehoto Awomi
Naga Army No. 4266, 11th Battalion,
4th Brigade, 2nd Division
Central Command, Naga Army

7. 2nd Lieutenant Lhousinyu Angami
6th Battalion, 2nd Brigade
1st Division, Southern Command
Naga Army

8. Sergeant Major Krutsolie Ziru
6th Battalion, 2nd Brigade
1st Division, Southern Command
Naga Army

9. Sergeant Honivi Yeptho
Naga Army No. 4742, 4th Brigade Staff
2nd Division, Central Command,
Naga Army.

10. Sergeant Tokim Tikhir
4th Brigade Staff, 2nd Division
Central Command, Naga Army.

11. Sergeant Renthungo Odyuo
17th Battalion, 6th Brigade.
2nd Division, Central Command,
Naga army

12. Sergeant Samatai Luikham
7th Battalion, 3rd Brigade
1st Division, Southern Command.
Naga Army.

13. Corporal Khamkhui Tangkhul
7th Battalion, 3rd Brigade
1st Division, Southern Command.
Naga Army.

14. Corporal Kahie Angami
4th Battalion, 2nd Brigade
1st Division, Southern Command
Naga Army

15. Corporal Pukhato Swu
14th Battalion, 5th Brigade
2nd Division, Central Command,
Naga Army.

16. Lance Corporal Tokiye Wotsa
Naga Army No. 4653, 12th Battalion,
4th Brigade, 2nd Division
Central Command, Naga Army.

17. Lance Corporal Kiyeto Sema
12th Battalion, 4th Brigade, 2nd Division
Central Command, Naga Army.

18. Private Kichotsing Sangtam
12th Battalion, 4th Brigade, 2nd Division
Central Command, Naga Army.

19. Private Sailanbo Liangmai
4th Battalion, 2nd Brigade
1st Division, Southern Command
Naga Army.

20. Private Rüzhükhrie Kense
6th Battalion, 2nd Brigade
1st Division, Southern Command
Naga Army.

21. Private Visiekhrie Kense
6th Battalion, 2nd Brigade
1st Division, Southern Command
Naga Army.

22. Private Resieto Kense
6th Battalion, 2nd Brigade
1st Division, Southern Command
Naga Army.

23. Private Shürhitso Metha
6th Battalion, 2nd Brigade
1st Division, Southern Command
Naga Army.

24. Private Soleo Piele
6th Battalion, 2nd Brigade
1st Division, Southern Command
Naga Army.

25. Private Pheluolhou Chase
6th Battalion, 2nd Brigade
1st Division, Southern Command
Naga Army.

26. Private Zuheto Chishi
Naga Army No. 4449, 12th Battalion
4th Brigade, 2nd Division
Central Command, Naga Army

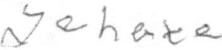

27. Private Yehaxe Sumi
14th Battalion, 5th Brigade
2nd Division, Central Command,
Naga Army.

28. Private Lhoxuto Assumi
14th Battalion, 5th Brigade
2nd Division, Central Command,
Naga Army.

Kivito

29. Private Kivito Achumi
14th Battalion, 5th Brigade
2nd Division, Central Command,
Naga Army.

PU KHALU

30. Private Pukhalu (Akhalu) Assumi
14th Battalion, 5th Brigade
2nd Division, Central Command,
Naga Army.

31. Private Salumo Sheqhi
14th Battalion, 5th Brigade
2nd Division, Central Command,
Naga Army.

32. Private Ivulho Lohe
14th Battalion, 5th Brigade
2nd Division, Central Command,
Naga Army.

33. Private Ghujuhe Futhena
14th Battalion, 5th Brigade
2nd Division, Central Command,
Naga Army.

12/08/2019

34. Private Vihoqhe Sumi
4th Brigade Staff, 2nd Division
Central Command, Naga Army.

Acknowledgements

Words are inadequate to pay the debts of gratitude I owe my heavenly Father; the ever-loving God. Thank you, Father, for all the happiness, the good times, and the dark days I battled through in my life. Thank you for enabling me to successfully complete this book.

Before I proceed further, I must thank my wonderful wife, Satemlila Imchen. The book was written during one of the darkest and most desperate periods of our lives, yet she encouraged and supported me by shouldering the entire responsibilities of the family, right from the start to the end, so that I could pursue my passion. Thank you so much dear, for placing your trust in me.

To Sergeant Honivi Yeptho, Private Zuheto Chishi, 2nd Lieutenant Zhehoto Awomi, and 2nd Lieutenant Yekhalu Jimo, on whose records, oral and written, I based my research footing. Without you, this book would never have been made possible today. To Sergeant Tokim Tikhir and Captain Sanguto Chase, who always gave their time to clarify my doubts and provided all the valuable information I needed. I am also grateful to all the other veterans for their support and co-operation during my research. May the Nagas recognize and acknowledge the sacrifices you made for them. Thank you, daring heroes.

To Mrs. Eustar Chishi Swu, President, Council of Nagalim Churches (CNC) NSCN-IM, for providing vital information on her husband, Late Isak Chishi Swu, former Yaruiwo, NSCN-IM. I extend my profound gratitude to Mrs. Chishi, a staunch revolutionary and God-fearing lady, for sparing her valuable time for me.

To everyone at team Maurice Wylie Media: Rev. Maurice Wylie, the ever-patient, kind and jolly managing director, his lady wife Mrs Maureen Wylie, a highly spiritual person; the whole creative team, including editors, proofreader and designers for their expertise, editorial support and guidance. I am eternally grateful for recognising and promoting the book to an international readership.

I am immensely indebted to Mr. Mughavi Chishi and Mrs. Hoinali Chishi for sponsoring the book. Mughavi has always been a friend, guide, and a brother to me; the man I could count on for the publication of the book. Thank you so much for being available whenever I needed you.

To my friend and a brother: a gifted poet and author of *The Dancing Quill* and *A Diamond of Dust*, Mr. A. Anato Swu, for connecting me to Maurice Wylie Media.

To the Sumi patriotic song band 'Sümi Sheshu,' for allowing me to use their original sound, 'Sumi war cry' in the video trailer of the book.

To all those who contributed to the successful completion of the book: Mr. H. Akaito Sema, Mrs. Neila Ayemi, Mr. and Mrs. Ayito H. Yeptho, Mr. and Mrs. Kavi Swu, Mr. and Mrs. Raju Regmi, Miss Shikani S. Aye, Mr. Pilato Wotsa, Mrs and Er. I. Hokiye Zhimo, and my sister-in-law Ms. Akanglemla Imchen. A line for you - I shall always cherish the roles you played.

I have to conclude by thanking my in-laws, Mr. & Mrs. A. Ajem Imchen, for their constant encouragement and support.

Pekingto Y. Jimo

Preface

For over thirty years, in a small village in Nagaland, India, a farmer would often narrate to his son the unforgettable memories of a Mission in which he had participated as a young man. I grew up listening to the stories of the Naga Army Mission to China. My father's never-ending stories always fascinated me and I always longed to write a book; but my dreams were far from being achieved due to lack of time and resources. The thought of not being able to portray the hardships borne by the patriots on that trip and the betrayal upon them kept haunting me ever since I was a young boy. However, by the grace of the Almighty God and the inspiration derived from my father, I decided to start writing this book. In 2018, I undertook the task with the intention of keeping those memories alive for the upcoming generations. I have invested all my available efforts to put every detail into action. After the publication of the book, I am hopeful that the world will come to know about the love, sacrifices, and the betrayal upon the Naga patriots of the Mission.

As I set about my research on the story, I began to realise that there was no book or written statements which contained the truth and a complete record of the Mission. I can assure that I have collected enough reliable and first-hand information and materials that debunk what many Nagas have falsely claimed. I also assure that this is the book that will clear certain accusations labelled against the Naga patriots by some vested Naga individuals.

In the course of my research, I stumbled upon a faded letter duly signed by Mr. Isak Chishi Swu, the President's Special Envoy to China and written by his Personal Secretary addressed to an injured veteran who was left in a foreign land. The letter aided me in ascertaining certain important dates of battles where at least nine Naga Army soldiers lost their lives fighting the Burmese Special Forces in Burma land (Myanmar).

Of the 312 men who had participated in the mission, just a little over a hundred men were alive by the time I could trace them. During my research, I interviewed forty-five veterans across the state, including some from a neighbouring state. I am still in contact with many of them.

They have all shared their stories and records with me as to how they were deceitfully betrayed into the enemy's hand by their own; how they returned to find their wives and fiancées had already belonged to others; how their parents and loved ones were long gone when they finally returned home; how they were rejected and left forgotten by the very people for whom they gave their everything.

So moving and exemplary are their sacrifices and love for their motherland that I felt these heroes deserve recognition and respect. I, therefore, determined myself to tell their story to the Nagas and to the world through this book, *"The Lost Mission."*

Abbreviations Used

- Brig. Brigadier
- Bde. Brigade
- Bn. Battalion
- CC Central Command
- CSM Command Sergeant Major
- Col. Colonel
- ENRC Eastern Naga Revolutionary Council
- FGN Federal Government of Nagaland
- GHQ General Headquarters
- Gen. General
- GPRN Government of the People's Republic of Nagaland
- HQ Headquarter
- KIA Kachin Independence Army
- NNC Naga National Council
- NA Naga Army
- NSCN National Socialist Council of Nagaland
- PLA People's Liberation Army
- Pte. Private
- RGN Revolutionary Government of Nagaland
- SC Southern Command

CHAPTER 1

The Road to China

"The blood we give today is for your liberty, a free and a sovereign Naga land. In honour will our leaders struggle in poverty; but never for a petty fortune will they have us betrayed."

Strongly convinced that the Nagas would uphold their acts of valour and sacrifices, they accepted the order for a perfidious mission to China. Why should one live in fear and uneasiness as though somebody from a close quarter watches his every movement?

Therefore, on December 8th, 1967, 312 brave men of the 1st and the 2nd Divisions of the Naga Army led by Isak Chishi Swu, Foreign Secretary, NNC and General Mowu Gwizantsu, Commander-in-Chief, Naga Army, embarked on a foreign trip to free from an alien grip the land they hold so dear.

Probing the border area

Before the Command was sent off, top brass officers felt it was indispensable for the government to find the easiest and shortest route to China. Finding Tikhir area as an ideal location, Sergeant Tokim Tikhir of 4th Brigade Staff was tasked with the assignment to probe the border area. He was just 20 years of age when assigned with the duty. Sergeant Tokim Tikhir of Pokhpur village was only 15 when he was conscripted into the 1st Brigade (later reassigned as 4th Brigade) of Naga Army in the March of 1962.

That gusty day, Sergeant Tokim, along with two of his men, Private Khiungakiu Tikhir of Anadangrü village and Private Phanongkhiu Tikhir of Shamator, set about surveying the terrain to locate the easiest route for the Command. They also took note of enemy positions and the activities of Assam Rifles who were manning the Pokhpur and Thongsonyu posts at the Indo-Burma international border.

Sergeant Tokim Tikhir, a brave soldier and an orator, could instill a great sense of nationalism in the minds of village chiefs and youths, so that many of them were even enlisted for the command as new recruits to be trained in China. The chiefs assured them that guides, rations and all other logistic support that they would depend upon on their journey would be provided. His operational success, however, was aided greatly and ensured to some extent by the unflinching support provided by the two brave and sincere Privates.

Mercenaries sent to assassinate

By October 1967, intelligence reports cautioned that certain mercenaries had been tasked to assassinate Isak Chishi Swu, and were stalking him in order to prevent him from reaching out to China.

Isak Chishi Swu, therefore, requested Lieutenant Colonel Salumo, Commander of the 14th Battalion Headquarters of Mukalimi, to detail his men to escort him to safety and to China thereafter.

At times like that, it was the 14th Battalion which had men he could trust. The Foreign Secretary who hailed from Chishilimi village totally trusted the men of 14th Battalion based at Mukalimi village. It is to be noted that the two villages are situated within close proximity, under Pughoboto Sub-Division.

A family man at heart

On an October day of 1967, Lieutenant Colonel Salumo of Ighanumi, commander of the 14th Battalion, called for an officers' emergency meeting with Captain Akhalu of Lazami, Commander of 24th Company,

Captain Ghilekha Awomi of Mishilimi, Captain Ghunakha of Ghokimi, Lieutenant Inakhe of Ighanumi and 2nd Lieutenant Yekhalu of Lizumi, 2 I/C of the 24 Company.

"Gentlemen, we have received an order to escort our Foreign Secretary to China on a Diplomatic Mission and I have chosen Captain Akhalu, Commander of the 24th Company to lead our men," announced Lieutenant Colonel Salumo Sumi.

"I am glad, Sir, to be a part of any foreign trip; but with due respect, Sir, may I speak a word?" requested Captain Akhalu. "Sir, I am having my daughter married before long," he continued.

"I am but a family man with no experience of foreign trips as yet; but my 2 I/C 2nd Lieutenant Yekhalu Jimo, with his trip to East Pakistan (Present day Bangladesh) along with General Zuheto Swu, has one such experience under his belt, and he is a young, sincere and daring officer. May I therefore, recommend him for the mission?" requested the Captain.

All the officers present consented and commissioned the Lieutenant for the mission. 2nd Lieutenant Yekhalu Jimo happily accepted the responsibility. But he never knew that he was leaving behind his fiancée, whom he may never get to marry.

On the 30th of October, 1967, the 14th Battalion men, under the command of Second Lieutenant Yekhalu Jimo escorted Mr. Isak Chishi Swu out of its jurisdiction to the 4th Brigade headquarters at Chomi village in Pungro circle of Kiphrie district of Nagaland, bordering Myanmar. The Commander and his 37 loyal and brave men, unaware of the never-returning journey, embarked on the mission in such ecstasy that they would not even bother to bid a proper adieu to the camp they so adored.

Little did they know that they were in fact bidding a final goodbye to their camp at Mukalimi as they left their home behind for a perilous journey ahead, that fateful day beneath dark and stormy skies.

Where is Mr Chishi?

By the time they neared Mudutsugho, a hamlet in Satakha sub-division, dusk had fallen. The skies' gloomy darkness had begun to overshadow the faint lights that emanated from the houses of the village. The advance guard wanted to enter the village; but Isak ordered, "Young men, avoid the village and move straight ahead to the woods. There we shall rest."

The men therefore rerouted their course, strategically crossed the Kohima road on the outskirts of the village, and moved up to the mountains. In the woods, between Vishepu and Mudutsugho villages, while they rested, Isak spoke to the commander of the Battalion, 2nd Lieutenant Yekhalu Jimo.

"Lieutenant, I want you to go back to the village and fetch me Mr Huskha Chishi. You can take along a unit, select men of your choice." "Okay, Sir"

"When you find him, you must tell him that I have sent you for him and he will understand. Tell him that his brother desires his company on a journey to a foreign land." "Yes, Sir"

"We shall await your return, not here; but by the road before Vishepu village. I believe you are clear with night's password?"

"No worries, Sir," replied the officer confidently, and left for the village with Sergeant Major Inavi, Private Piwoto, Private Xukiye and nine others. The Lieutenant and his men cautiously walked down the wild nut-filled hills to the village, approached the man's house and moved in; but the man was not at home.

In the wee hours, when the Lieutenant and his men returned to the column, they had to go through a vital yet slightly disturbing moment with the duty guard before they could relax their tired selves.

"Halt! Who is there?"

"Easy, comrade, it's us."

"Password, please."

"Ayepu" (Star)

"Oh Sir, welcome back!"

"Thank you, soldier" said the Lieutenant, patted the soldier's back, and walked up straight to Isak to report the details.

"I am sorry, Sir; the man was not at home. We even probed the village secretly and found out that he was out of the village." "Alas! I am unlucky. I wanted to work with him. Lieutenant, you and your men must be tired. Go take some rest and we shall resume the walk early."

"Sleep well, Sir." "You too, Lieutenant"

Isak Chishi Swu so wanted Mr Huskha to accompany him to China. The man was one of the highly qualified and knowledgeable intellectuals of the time; perhaps the reason Mr Isak had desired his companionship.

The General's delay

At Chomi, the Central Command awaited the arrival of General Mowu Gwizantsu and his men of Southern Command. They had waited for a month when General Mowu failed to reach Chomi village within the stipulated time.

On the other hand, General Mowu was at Peace Camp, Chedema, pleading with the FGN leaders to expedite the process and issue the command order at the earliest opportunity. The General had already instructed Captain Sanguto Chase, one of his trusted men and a brave officer, to reach 9th Battalion Headquarters at Phugwima village along with 80 brave men of GHQ Pfuchi.

The kiss of a lover

At about seven o'clock in the evening of 5th December 1967, while sitting by the fireside with Isak Chishi Swu and a few other guards at 4th Brigade HQ, Lieutenant Yekhalu took the chance to seek a special permission.

"Sir, if you please; may I speak a word with you?" "Yes, you may, Lieutenant; tell me, what is it?"

"Sir, I seek your permission to go to Zunheboto to meet my parents." "But why?"

"Sir, I must go and get some cash, because back at the Battalion headquarter, we did not receive any money; and with these many men on such a long journey, I must, as their commander, have some cash with me." "See, officer, I absolutely understand your problem; but keeping in mind the current situation, it is a little too risky, both for you and the command, to let you go home at such a time as this."

"But with due respect, Sir, I must go home; for if I don't, my men may suffer during the mission. We are all completely out of cash, we are just marching without prior notice, we were given no time at all; you are well aware of it, Sir."

Isak silently pulled out his notepad from his coat pocket, scribbled down a note, tore it off and handed it over to the Lieutenant. "Alright, officer, here's your permission. Go get your work done; but get back to the camp within five days, for any day in a week's time, we may have to move out."

"Thank you so very much Sir; and yes, I shall return before the given period of time, Sir."

The next morning, beneath the red and yellow autumn foliage that glittered like gold in the bright morning sunrays, chirpings songs of autumn birds echoed through the hills and dales. A gentle breeze was blowing through the slender pine trees and its evergreen needles. A fair-complexioned, compact and fairly handsome and excited young man in his early thirties, with a countenance beaming with delight, cheerfully walks home.

As he double-timed through the verdant meadows and the undulating hills, the babbling and burbling sound of a stream could be heard. A harvested paddy field and the smooth flowing rivers curving gently through the hills and jungles reminded him of home.

Soon enough, the Lieutenant, on the wings of cupid, was flown to the most beautiful place in his village; the thatched, wooden cottage of his fiancée.

"Ilomi, (my dear) how rude and unlucky the girl and the parents who refused your parents' proposal must be, to refuse your relationship just for the sake of your being illiterate. I mean, what could have so blinded them that they failed to see through your beautiful heart, your handsomeness, your smartness, your bravery, your kindness? It goes on and on and I would still not be satisfied praising you my dear. Oh! How lucky I must be to be your lover!"

"Thank you, ilomi, I am lucky as well," calmly replied the lieutenant.

"I am here by your side to make them regret," assured his fiancée.

"Nothing in the world matters as long as I have you. You are my world, my strength and my weakness; you are my everything, dear. Thank you for loving this poor fellow."

"I shall be with you to the end of the world and if heaven permits, I shall be your love even beyond death," soothed his fiancée.

"As long as I shall live, I shall always keep you happy and forever loved."

"Oh dear, and here's the akho (a traditional conical shaped basket crafted of cane or bamboo culms with straps used for carrying rice grains and such other things) you gifted me. I don't let anyone use it even when I am off to school. Oh, and by the way; I saw your younger brother wearing the shawl I had woven for you. Do you not like it, my dear?" curiously asked the Lieutenant's fiancée.

"But in the jungles when do I get to wear it, my love? The brightness of the shawl will wear off pretty quickly and also its beauty, so I left it with my brother. Why would I not love a gift from you, Ilomi?"

"Oh My God, look at the sky, dear! The darkened horizon: there's a raging storm fast approaching. Just wait here; I'll go get the clothes."

The words 'raging storm' broke his reverie, and the Lieutenant soon found himself caught in the middle of rumbling thunder. In a trice, a strong wind rushed across the mountains and the rain that lashed down, left the Lieutenant completely drenched there in the hills, far from home.

Lieutenant Yekhalu halted for the night at Khukishe village and, treading the murky terrains, reached Zunheboto, his home town, the next day. As he headed for his village, the Lieutenant met his uncle (father's younger brother) on the way on the outskirts of Zunheboto town.

"Yekhalu, son, at this hour! How did you get home, my son?" asked his surprised uncle.

"Ipu, (used both for uncle and father), disclose it not even to my parents or fiancée; I am on a mission to a foreign land and I need money, so I am heading to the village to borrow some from my fiancée." "My son, just yesterday, I saw her going to a conference at Bhaimho village along with the church members."

"I must go there, then." "Here's 25 rupees I have with me, take it and go in Christ, my son. May the good Lord be with you."

"Thank you Ipu, take care" said the Lieutenant, and headed for Bhaimho, a village three to four kilometres away from Zunheboto town where the Sumi Baptist Churches Annual Convention was being held from 7th to 10th December 1967. At Bhaimho village, the Lieutenant with the help of the conference volunteers, could soon track his fiancée's campsite.

"Oh, my dear, what has brought you here? Oh, I am so very happy to see you."

"Ilomi, I need some money very urgently, I would be happy if you could lend me some."

"I am so sorry, Ilomi, I don't have any at the moment; but where are you going and why in such a hurry?"

"I must reach the camp as early as possible and I cannot tarry much longer, but I promise I am coming back and we shall then get married."

"Oh Ilomi, I do not know where you are going and when you shall be coming back; but this I promise: no matter how long, you shall find me there, still waiting for you when we next meet."

"Will you still be there for me, my love?" asked the Lieutenant.

"Yes, my dear, I will forever wait for our union."

"If possible, please stay back for some more days, dear. I have an unusually strange sense of fear. I don't know why; but this time I have this strange feeling that I might lose you."

"Oh, dear, stop being silly! I must go; and do not worry, nothing will happen. We shall soon be together forever."

"Be back soon, your love shall eagerly await your return. Farewell, my love."

Yekhalu just looked into his fiancée's eyes intently, kissed her on the forehead, and left without saying a word.

I must say "No!"

General Hokiye approached the headquarters of 4th brigade without any prior information and got into a little trouble in getting past the Shiphi outpost, which was manned by mission men under the command of 2nd Lieutenant Zhehoto Awomi of 11th and 2nd Lieutenant Yetovi of 14th Battalions.

"Officers, this is General Hokiye. I am on an urgent mission and I must meet your brigade commander immediately. Open the gate and let my men pass through," ordered General Hokiye Swu.

"No disrespect, General Sir, but I am sorry we cannot allow you unless we receive a confirmation from the Brigadier himself," replied 2nd Lieutenant Zhehoto Awomi.

"We have been given strict order that none without the knowledge of the brigade commander be permitted to pass the outpost," added 2nd Lieutenant Yetovi Sumi.

"You must do it. That is an order. Defy my order and you shall bear the consequences!" fumed the General.

The two officers ordered their men to take positions and shouted back, "We shall lay down our lives here if we must, but never shall we let you pass this point without our commander's order."

They finally allowed the General and his men to enter the camp after the confirmation from Brigadier Kivihe reached them. The General was not happy with the two officers initially, but later appreciated them for performing their duty without fear and holding on to the commander's order under any circumstances.

As Sergeant Honivi read out 2nd Lieutenant Zhehoto's letter which had arrived from the outpost stating General Hokiye's visit, Brigadier Kivihe immediately said to Asu Isak: "Quick, keep yourself from the General's sight."

"General Hokiye made every effort to convince Brigadier Kivihe; but every time the General pulled his chair closer to him, the Brigadier would move farther from the General and kept abstaining from hearing what the General had wanted to say or offer. Finally, the Brigadier's resolute decision made the General leave the camp disappointed," recounted Sergeant Honivi Yeptho.

Mercenaries' hunt for Isak intensified. He therefore had to sail under false colours for over a month even in the 4th brigade area, in the Chomi region of Nagaland.

Sergeant Tokim narrated how he, in order to shield Isak's identity from the people in his village, had to manufacture lies that Isak was a class eight passed new recruit who was assigned as his secretary.

In their heart was desertion

While they were still at Chomi, the Central Command came under a heavy strain from certain sections of Naga Army, which had deviated from the mainstream. With numerous offers from their adversaries and being ill prepared for such a tough journey, some Naga Army could not resist deserting the command.

Eleven Naga Army soldiers led by Lieutenant Longrie Tangkhul deserted the command. They were pursued and ambushed by the command men; five of them were caught by Corporal Yehoto Jimo, unit Clerk of 12th Battalion, and his men who had waylaid them. The captured were all left at the 10th Headquarters.

At another time, Private Ghilekha of Mishilimi and Private Sheniyi of Ighanumi, both belonging to the 14th deserted the command. They were captured and handed over to the men at the 10th Headquarters at Hotsur.

Meanwhile, two Lance Corporals and seven Privates of 12th Battalion, viz. Private Lutoyi Sumi of Khukishe village, Private Jenihe Sumi of Khukishe village, Private Yetoje Yeptho of Sukhalu village, Private Hekiye Sumi of Vedami village, Private Heshito Sumi of Kulhopu village, Private Xetoi Sumi of Lukhuyi village, Private Vitoje Sumi of Sheipu village and Private Tojevi Sumi of Ghokhuvi village, led by Lance Corporal Tokiye Wotsa and Lance Corporal Luvishe Sumi of Saghemi, deserted the command to join hands with the soldier band of the Army Government founded by General Kaito Sukhai.

They were on their way to 13th Battalion HQ where Army Government was camping, when they were caught by the command men from Satami village and handed over to the command at Chomi.

Lance Corporal Kiyeto Sema, who was closely associated with the brigade commander, recounted how he pleaded with Brigadier Kivihe to spare his brother Vitoje Jimo from being punished.

"Brigadier, Sir, may I request you to kindly spare my brother, Private Vitoje from being punished."

"All of them are receiving the severest of punishment and nobody escapes, not even your brother," fumed the Brigadier as he turned his head away.

"But Sir, they have all realised their mistakes, and these are good and tough soldiers, they will prove it for sure; not just my brother, but you may please forgive them all," Kiyeto pleaded again.

"Kiyeto, do you mean you can even risk your life for these soldiers? What if, any of them betrays us again; will you die on their behalf?"

"Yes, Sir, I would," answered Kiyeto, overpowered with the emotions of saving his brother's life and also having complete faith in his battalion comrades.

"We were considered for the mission because we honestly confessed that we had deserted, not to surrender before the Indian Army but to join the Army Government in another Naga outfit, newly formed by General Kaito Sukhai," explained Lance Corporal Tokiye Wotsa.

They believed it was just another Naga Army. However, they displayed extreme loyalty and dedication throughout the entire Mission.

When one day turns to twenty days

As they awaited General Mowu and his men at Chomi, the secret of their Mission had already leaked out and the Indian Army had taken extra measures at the borders to prevent their exit into a foreign land. The Assam Rifles of Pokhpur post and Thongsonyu post had tightened their security by securing the posts with more personnel pouring in. In just one day alone, choppers dropped Indian Army soldiers fourteen times. This later caused the Naga Army to walk 20 days to reach the 139th international pillar at the Indo-Myanmar border: a feat which could have been accomplished in just a day, had they taken the Pokhpur village road.

General Mowu's arrival was way behind schedule. Leaving Isak Chishi Swu with no other option but to launch the command operation ahead of his arrival. Therefore, Central Command under Isak Chishi Swu on the night of December 6, 1967, left Chomi for 10th HQ at Hotsur; halted there a day, and before the Assam Rifles at Phokhungri could detect their movements, sneaked out of Nagaland for China on 8th December 1967. They crossed Phokhungri area into Sutso village, rested for a while at the River Tiho, then walked into the jungles of Mimi.

As they navigated the hostile dales and hills, casting their eyes at the distant snow-capped peaks of Saramati and left their home for a foreign land, Private Zuheto Chishi of 12th in tears sings a song.

Dark and Gloomy Snow

Oh Snow, behold a soldier, far-off bound,
And if thou may, do spare me from thy doom,
For thou art mindful of my trek homebound;
I flee but never can outrun thy gloom.

How dreadful art thou, dark and gloomy Snow!
Oh, how far from thee can this doomed soul flee?
And if to die, this heart so surely know,
Why then must this soul live in fear of thee?

And though today from thee make I my flight,
For sure, to thee must this poor soul return,
And in thy lying beauty take delight,
Ere enter I the sovereign realm I yearn.

Oh Snow, to thy cold paths must I return
Ere enter I the sovereign realm I yearn.

"If not for these words, it would have been a complete disaster listening to such a horrific voice," jocularly mocked Sergeant Honivi Yeptho. For a while, in laughter they continued their march; but the Private walked with sombre expression overshadowing his otherwise cheerful visage.

It's time to bomb the fish

On the other hand, General Mowu Gwizantsu and his men of Southern Command, numbering 150 Naga Army men, moved out from 9th Battalion HQ Phugwima on the 1st December 1967. Unlike the Central Command men, most men of the Southern Command were unaware of the Mission on which they were embarking, with the exception of a few officers like Captain Sanguto; yet they obeyed the order and marched in dauntless allegiance.

On the fateful afternoon of 8th December 1967, as they rested for tea at the banks of the river Tizu, soldiers, enthralled by the abundance of the fishes in the water, sought the General's permission to bomb it, but he refused.

"General Sir, please allow us to bomb the river," pleaded the General's men for the second time.

The General, daring yet kind by nature allowed them but not without a caution, "Just two sticks, and be careful, for the waters could prove disastrous."

As the soldiers excitedly dived into the river, the dark and the angry waters picked the first victim of the Mission. Private Mhalevo of 6th from Chiechama village did not resurface. He became the first man of the Mission to perish, leaving his comrades to mourn his death with a sad and apprehensive song.

> Oh waters, dark and cold;
> All that breathes, young and old,
> Must sink before thy feet,
> Because thou none can cheat.

His comrades retrieved his body the next morning and buried him there at the river bank. There, in the unmarked grave on the banks of Tizu river, lies a Naga hero, more precious than gold and silver. That unhappy corner, made pleasant by the mortal remains of Private Mhalevo, shall forever remain sacred in our hearts.

The 2nd Lieutenant Yekhalu, who was returning from Zunheboto, also arrived at the river the same day and marched along with the General's men to Chomi. Unfortunately, Isak and his men had already left and he was pushed to the brink of missing the mission when Brigadier Kivihe Swu denied him permission to let him walk alongside General Mowu: "I am sorry Lieutenant, but I cannot allow you to walk any further alongside General Mowu and his men."

"But all my arms and baggage have been carried off and my battalion men are marching without their commander," pleaded Lieutenant Yekhalu.

"I am afraid you are a little too late for the Mission." "With due respect, Sir, you must consider the case. I was granted a special leave by the Foreign Secretary himself. Here's the permission note he gave me," said the Lieutenant, and handed over the letter.

Destiny finally smiled upon the Lieutenant. Isak's handwritten note that he had carried served as his ticket to China.

Nothing, ever, could have equalled the joy he must have felt that moment. A man from the narrow footpaths of a hamlet in a corner of Nagaland is ready to set out for China, many a hundred miles away from home. His happiness overshadowed the doom that prowled in the treks ahead.

"Okay, Lieutenant, you and Captain Itokhu of 11th Battalion can go with General Mowu and his men," said Brigadier Kivihe Swu.

Troops were added

On the other side, Isak and his men reached Mütungrü on 9th December. There, seven members of ENRC viz. Tusangchu Longpfürr, Lensüthong Mukori, Rhichin Longpfürr, Zhinkho Longpfürr, Nupentsü Longpfürr, Khotsea Longpfürr, Mongchü Longpfürr and Pensuchü Makuri joined them; all fresh recruits to be trained in China.

Here, they rested a day, arranged their food supplies and moved on to Ningshet, the village they reached on 11th December. The next day, they arrived at Nükrük which, in Khiamniungan dialect, is also known as Tang village.

We are Phizo's Army

On 13th December, the Central Command arrived upon a big village in the Phuluntong range, the village where the practice of morung and beating of log drums was still prevalent. Their presence in the village was alerted by the resonating sounds of the log drum which the guard manning the duty had sounded. Before long, they were surrounded from all sides by the villagers with traditional weapons and were prepared to fight them. Soon the chief arrived and questioned them.

"The chief enquires about our identity, Sir," Raju Peyu Vihoshe, the command translator said to Isak Chishi Swu.

The translator listened as Isak spoke to him and then replied to the chief, "We are Phizo's Army, oh chief." The chief, on hearing the name Phizo, signalled his warriors to stay calm and ordered food to be arranged for the men. He later narrated a past event, where A. Z. Phizo in his visit had requested them to support and guide any Army that comes in his name. Angami Zapu Phizo was the then President of Naga National Council, who had fled Nagaland and lived in exile in London.

As a sign of hospitality and respect, the chief presented Isak Chishi Swu with eggs as special food, while Isak reciprocated with a Naga shawl and money. The chief was so pleased, that he even sent messengers to the others villages that the command would be passing, advising that they should support and guide Phizo's Army to their destination.

The next day, they left the village with the guide the chief arranged for them, and reached Langnok, a Khiamniungan village, on 14th December, 1967, reached Heikong, a Leinong Naga village, on 15th. They arrived at Anpu, another Leinong village, Nagas of Burma on 16th December, and from this village, they walked the whole night to Solonokcheu village.

CHAPTER 2
The First Battle

Walking the whole night, Isak and his men reached Solonokcheu village early in the morning of December 17th, 1967. By this time the command was already fatigued through lack of sleep and the night's walk.

Solonokcheu is a Leinong Naga village. It lies in the Tezok range under Lahe Township in Burma. It literally means a small village that migrated from Solo, which, among the Leinong Nagas is known as Solonoknyu.

Burma village bids us welcome

Upon reaching the village, Sergeant Major Inavi Tsuqu and Private Pukhalu Assumi of 14th Battalion, who were among the men leading the vanguard that day, were sent into the village to ascertain the situation. When they inquired the presence of Burmese forces, the villagers told them that the Burmese forces had since long stopped patrolling the area. They happily ate food from a house, bought rice and vegetables for themselves and reported to the command that they were safe from the hands of the enemy.

Securing the perimeter

The command positioned itself and secured perimeters with 14th men at the main bunker, flanked by 11th as advance guard support on the west, and 12th as reserve on the east positions. However, relying heavily on the comforting news of the villagers, they relaxed themselves without much alertness. Some of them even strolled around the village like gentlemen of leisure; unaware of loads of work the Mission had piled up for them. Private Akhalu recalls, "Sergeant Major Inavi and I laid down at the fireside and took a leisure nap while most of our comrades were busy husking rice grain with which they were issued; but a few hours later in the afternoon, I woke to the sounds of gunshots."

Burmese surprise attack

Around 2 to 3 o'clock in the afternoon, a Burmese troop sneaked through the first bunker manned by the 14th and 11th Battalion men and surprised the ill-prepared Naga Army with their ferocious attack.

Out of exhaustion and relying completely on the reports of the villagers, the soldiers of 14th Battalion left the post without much care. They had even left their guns at the post, entrusting the 11th Battalion men to take care of them.

An ill wind blew into the 14th men, for in the attack they suffered an embarrassing loss of a Light Machine Gun and a Mark III rifle into the enemy's hands. The men displayed immaturity and indiscipline; but having learnt a tough lesson, the men later proved themselves an asset to the command. Records support the fact that most of the 14th men displayed great courage and seized as many as ten arms, including two LMG (Light Machine Gun), the most captured enemy's arms in the command.

Sergeant Honivi's goose bumps

Meanwhile, at Captain Yeshiho's mess, which was positioned at the centre of the village; moments before firing began, a few Naga Army were calmly strolling around the village, while many were bathing.

Sergeant Honivi Yeptho, Clerk in 4th Brigade, was among those who had taken a bath. After he had finished bathing from a machang, he walked back to the kitchen, and as he sat by the fireside, three bullets coming from the way he had just entered, hit the roof above his head.

"It gave me goose bumps when I thought of how I could have been the target of those three shots had I lingered there at the door even for a short while. I surely could have been killed had I waited a little longer at the entrance. It's the grace of God that saved me that day," said the Sergeant.

Village man takes first bullet

Ready to take a bath, the bodyguard of Isak Chishi Swu, Sergeant Nihokhu Sumi of 14th Battalion, had just removed his shirt, when the owner of the house in which they were taking shelter, walked up the machang and offered him some dry fried seeds of creeping beans. But before he could relish the delicious beans, enemy shots reached them, and passed through the man's thigh. They both jumped down the machang, and while the Sergeant took cover, the man limped down the village slope howling in pain. He was later tracked down and his injury taken care of by the command men.

It's time to make the fake call

The men of the 11th also suffered the loss of a rifle and a 2-inch mortar. But before the Burmese could leave with the arms, 2nd Lieutenant Zhehoto Awomi and Sergeant Shikuto, the unit commander of 12th engaged the enemy with heavy firing from two sides, forcing the enemy to retreat without the snatched arms.

A witty officer, 2nd Lieutenant Zhehoto Awomi, promptly cried out a fake call for the launcher and LMG units to attack from the other side. "Launcher unit, LMG unit, charge, the enemy has gotten our arms," cried out the officer.

The call, however funny it might have sounded to the Nagas, was little known to the enemy. The Lieutenant's idea worked: it threw the enemy into utter panic and forced them to take cover, rather than focusing on the snatched arms. Sergeant Shikuto, swiftly rushed in with two of his boys and provided a vital covering fire.

"Lieutenant Sir, you are clear to go; go for the arms, we have your back," shouted the Sergeant as he continued firing with his men. 2nd Lieutenant Zhehoto bravely retrieved the 2-inch mortar and the rifle that had been snatched from the 11th Battalion.

"Let these arms be recorded as the enemy arms seized by 2nd Lieutenant Zhehoto Awomi of 11th and Sergeant Shikuto," declared Isak Chishi when the incident was reported.

Map retrieval

The element of surprise had taken its toll on the Naga Army when the 12th position was also attacked by the enemy. Soldiers here were strongly holding the line; however, some new recruits and a few others, displayed yet another disappointing performance riddled with errors and embarrassments. In the midst of chaos and run for cover, they had left the guide map behind, the only thing that would take them to their destination.

Corporal Nihozu of 11th displayed extreme courage when he lobbed hand grenades, while 2nd Lieutenant Zhehoto Awomi and Sergeant Jehoto Tsuruhumi gave covering shots and Sergeant Ihoshe, bodyguard of Isak Chishi Swu, all of the 11th swiftly crawled back and retrieved the map.

Taken captive

While running for cover, Private Khotsea Longpfürr of Hakhomüte village mistakenly ran into the enemy line and was taken captive. He was released later, when he told the Burmese forces that he was just conscripted into the Mission, and that he had not even received any military training. The man could not join the command and later died in the village.

Repositioning and holding the village

By the time the sun began to go down, the Burmese were forced to retire due to tough resistance by the Naga Army, and they were driven for over a klick[1] from the battle site. This time the command planned a strict and strategic formation, secured perimeters and held the village for two days. A group was repositioned as the advance guard on the northern part of the village towards the route they would take for China.

The men assigned, dug in and established their position in a sloping jungle, a few hundred metres above the river that flowed beyond the village. They spent the night there and retreated to the village the next morning.

Let us die fighting rather than live hiding

It is better to die fighting than to live hiding; this is a principle not valued by many. After repelling the enemy far from the village, the command regrouped. As they sat to ascertain the command's status, the command was dismayed to find that Private Tsinthong Tikhir of Chiliso village and Private Toripkiu Tikhir of Mütungrü village, both belonging to the 4th Brigade staff, had deserted the command.

One cannot fully blame them for the fact that they were fresh recruits, who were just too young to withstand the pain a mature soldier has to undergo. As a matter of fact, they were ill-prepared. Later, on their return journey from China, the command learnt that both the deserters reached their respective villages without any harm.

A cold icy December night

When dusk had arrived, Tusangchu Longpfürr and Rhichin Longpfürr who had gone astray from the command, found themselves in the middle of a barren jhum field. They battled the cold icy night of December huddling themselves together, the longest night of their lives.

By the time the sun next appeared, it was not the chirps of birds they heard, but the voices of Sumi soldiers calling, "Come on out, boys and comrades, we have repelled the enemy and the village has been secured

---

[1] The military uses metric measurements for maps and distances. Klick is short term for one kilometer which is about 5/8 of a mile.

since last evening;" but he and his friend Rhichin, still kept themselves hidden, until the last man of the few who had gone astray the previous night had walked past them. The two had actually presumed that it might have been a ruse to get them out of their hiding places.

General Mowu with Southern Command arrives

Around eight in the forenoon of 18th December, General Mowu Gwizantsu arrived with 150 brave men of Southern Command. Here, Captain Itokhu, and 2nd Lieutenant Yekhalu Jimo, also reported their arrival to the command authority and took control of their units.

The Command formation

Isak Chishi Swu and General Mowu worked out the command formation. With a prayer from Vihoshe Shohe, they assigned their duties. The Mission comprised two commands, the Central and the Southern. Therefore, Central Command was assigned as Group A and Southern Command as Group B.

Special envoy to China:	Isak Chishi Swu, Foreign Secretary, NNC/FGN
Command Commander:	General Mowu Gwizantsu, C-in-C, FGN, Naga Army
Command 2 I/C:	Colonel Lhouvicha Angami
Command Adjutant:	Captain Yeshiho Sumi 4th Brigade Staff
Adjutant 2 I/C:	Captain Neilao Angami 6th Battalion
CSM:	Lieutenant Megosazo Angami
Command Quarter Master:	Captain Gwovile Angami
Command QM 2I/C:	Captain Tsupichu Pochury
PS to C-in-C:	Secretary Honrie Muivah
PS to President Special Envoy:	2nd Lieut. Khukihe Shikhu
Chief Medical Officer:	Lieutenant Dr. Samson Luikham,
Command Chaplain:	Vihoshe Shohe, Raju Peyu

Group A
Commander:	Captain Itokhu of 11 Battalion
Adjutant:	Captain Kochu Pochury, 4th Brigade Staff
Group CSM:	2nd Lieutenant Yekhalu Jimo, 14 Battalion Commander
Group QM:	2nd Lieutenant Zhehoto Awomi, 11 Battalion Commander

Group B
Commander:	Lieutenant Kehokri 5th Battalion
Adjutant:	Captain Sanguto Chase 4th Battalion
Group CSM:	Lieutenant Khokoto Angami 4th Battalion
Group QM:	2nd Lieutenant Kiyeto Angami 5th Battalion

They were anticipating another assault from the Burmese troops but, apart from the attack, they were not even seen for the rest of the journey before they reached China. It was assumed that the Burmese forces did not re-engage because they were tipped off about the Southern Command trailing behind them. The command then left the village as soon as the command formation was completed.

CHAPTER 3
Strangers in a Brother's Land

It is an absolute misfortune that most Nagas of Nagaland are still in the dark about their fellow Nagas living in Myanmar. Worse still, it is a curse for the few who are aware and yet refuse to accept the truth. Some Nagas of Nagaland were and are made to believe that they alone are the actual Nagas and any Naga outside is no Naga. We have xenophobic mistrust of every Naga who is not a Nagaland Naga. On the contrary, we have miserably failed to realise that the Nagas are one and that we have our ancestral roots towards the land where our brothers in Myanmar are living.

The Nagas of India have reasons, however, to be grateful to the British Empire, as some might say, for handing over a free Nagas into the hands of India. One reason was that Nagas would have been left extremely neglected, unreached and uncared for by either of the countries, leaving the present Nagas in incomprehensible poverty and backwardness.

Great Britain must have wronged the Nagas. The Naga Memorandum, submitted to the Simon Commission in January 1929, had made abundantly clear the desire of the Nagas, and the consequences, should England choose to decide otherwise. It knew perfectly well that the land Nagas inhabited belonged to the Nagas since time immemorial, and that India had no reason whatsoever to claim it as her land.

The Nagas helped Great Britain, and even served as Labour Corps on the shores of France during WWI, from early 1917 to mid-1918. The

Nagas had therefore expected that the British government would consider their aspiration and desires to be left out of the union of India, to be a free nation. On the contrary, Great Britain left the Nagas with a foreign shackle and gifted them off to the covetous duo, India and Myanmar, leaving the Nagas devastated and massively divided and scattered.

The Naga Army of the Mission, despite being in the ancestral land owned by their own, had the strangest feelings and experiences one would have in a foreign land. There were times when the Nagas were betrayed into the hands of Burmese Forces. Incidents have been recorded, where Naga soldiers of the Mission were killed and their heads, hands and legs chopped off by our Naga brothers of Burma. It was not their fault, and none blame them, for they knew not that we were one. The artificial identities of India and Burma, was the chief cause that had prompted them to execute such brutal actions.

Christmas in a foreign land

It is an undeniable fact that celebrating a festive occasion in a foreign land is pure joy; but one cannot also disagree that it is an absolute agony for those in the midst of a war or a perilous mission.

As they approached another small village, cool hilly winds and a familiar landscape reminded them of festive tunes that echoed the blue hills back home. Melancholic cries of partridge and the hill birds flowing along with the cool breeze of that winter forenoon and the soulful songs of Great Barbet resonating the distant hills and dales below, transported them all back home to their villages.

Christmas, a time best spent with family members and loved ones, was near; and here they are in a strange land, overcome with acute nostalgia for Christmas back home. On Christmas morning, Isak Chishi Swu and General Mowu led the men in a prayer, and celebrated a brief but sweet and a melancholic Christmas at the bank of a rivulet below the village. That Christmas was a celebration mixed with fears and tears. Many still remember in pain, that Yule they spent in a foreign land, pining for their home.

A national movement hero

Waktham village was in the northern part, fairly far from their route; but Isak and General Mowu decided to move their men to the village, deviating from their mission route. The two leaders wanted to meet S. S. Khaplang, the vice Chairman of Eastern Naga Revolutionary Council, to seek his favour and advice as they passed through his jurisdiction.

Their entry into the village, however, was not a welcoming one. As they approached the village premises, the village guards, with traditional weapons, began to exhibit suspicious movements. They, therefore, adopted a strict formation and entered the gate very cautiously in threes. Waktham, a village situated in the Sagaing region of Myanmar, is home to the Hemi Naga tribe of Myanmar. Mr. S. S. Khaplang, one of the greatest Naga National Movement heroes, was a brave son of this village.

Your Christmas gift, Sir – 25 live rounds!

Isak Chishi Swu and General Mowu, along with their guards, headed straight to the house of Mr. S. S. Khaplang, the Vice Chairman of Eastern Naga Revolutionary Council (ENRC) and also a co-founder of the Naga Defence Force. These two Naga organisations were fighting for a free and sovereign Naga land in Burma. They were accorded a hearty welcome, and Isak Chishi Swu presented Mr Khaplang with a Mark III Rifle with 25 live rounds as a Christmas gift. Mr Khaplang also commissioned 30 of his men for the Mission with Brigadier Simon as their commander. They marched alongside the command until they reached 2nd Brigade HQ of Kachin Independence Army.

A New Year with a difference

If Christmas was spent in a land away from home and still very far off from the destination, can New Year be celebrated at home? They walked throughout the old year's last day, and by the time they reached a Pangmi Naga village called Chaingraing, they had already walked past midnight into the New Year's Day of 1968. Captain Sanguto Chase and his comrade Lieutenant Megosazo of 4th Battalion, who were the rear-guard of the day, reached the village as late as one o'clock in the morning. They had to exchange New Year wishes while they were still walking on the way.

Chaingraing is a Tangshang Naga village under Nanyun township of Khamti District in Sagaing region, Myanmar. There they celebrated New Year, 1968, at a small church in the village. In a prayer, Isak Chishi prayed for the command's safe passage into China and as was his nature, he prayed for the protection of everyone from harm. It was said that Isak would pray every day at noon.

They rested the whole day in the village.

Warning at Ngalang village

On 6th January 1968, they came upon Ngalang, another Pangmi Naga village situated on the bank of a river. The village had abundance of sugarcane plants and cassava plants of both the red and white peels. Here they were warned that consumption of tapioca mixed with sugarcane juice on an empty stomach was injurious to health. However, some of them were too hungry to heed the warning, and, in a hurry to satiate their hunger, many of them hurriedly peeled the tapioca and ate it half roasted. As expected, most of those who ate it suffered severe dysentery.

Sumi woman in Ngalang

At one mess, the Sumis of Central Command were surprised to hear a woman in Burma speaking to them in Sumi. "Oh, I can hardly believe my eyes! How is it possible that these many Sumis are here in our village!" exclaimed the lady. "Rather, it is we who are surprised to see a Sumi woman in Burma," revealed the Nagas.

The lady explained that she was a Sumi married to a Pangmi Naga man of the village, and she hailed from Chief Zuhovi's village Longtong, on the far northern end of Ledu road. Longtong is a Sumi village, in Tinsukia District of Assam. On being told of the Mission, the woman gifted them with a hen. She also took them to her house and prayed for them. But amidst the joy that tarried for a while, homesickness soon crept up on them; and, as she spoke, their hearts began to beat faster. They could see their mothers in her visage of cheerfulness. They were overcome with an acute nostalgia for their days at home with their mothers. "We thanked her and bade goodbye," narrated 2nd Lieutenant Yekhalu, while Private Kivito Achumi, of Natsumi, belonging to 14th recounted how the village folks were merrymaking that day.

Leave no one behind

Private Khumtsa, a brave young boy from Lazami village, under Pughoboto, was assigned to 14th Battalion, 5th Brigade, 2nd Division, Central Command, Naga Army, before he was commissioned for the command. In the Mission, he was attached to the President's Special Envoy as his attendant, along with four others from his Battalion who were assigned as Isak's Bodyguards, viz., Private Kivito Achumi of Natsumi, Private Xukiye Sumi of Iphonumi, Private Akhalu Shikhu of Lazami and Sergeant Nihokhu Sumi of Chishilimi.

Private Khumtsa was among those who suffered from dysentery, but his turned out to be fatal. He felt too ill to walk by himself. Isak Chishi even tried giving his own personal food and medicines, but to no avail.

That was when he called 2nd Lieutenant Yekhalu Jimo, the unit commander of 14th and asked him, "Lieutenant, what shall we do with the man?" "Sir, your call shall be final; but if you still seek my opinion, I intend to carry the Private along, for I do not wish to see any of my men left behind," expressed 2nd Lieutenant Yekhalu.

The Lieutenant was hopeful that the Private had a fighting chance of pulling through, so he ordered his men to carry the Private along. They carried him along on a makeshift bamboo stretcher as they walked beside the stream until they reached a mountain.

Private Tsumongthong disappears

Sergeant Tokim Tikhir plaintively narrated how he and his company men had gone deep into the jungles of a virgin forest in search of their comrade Private Tsumongthong Tikhir of Anadangrü village. It was on the 9th day of January 1968. While in the forest, they settled down to cook their meal. Private Tsumongthong Tikhir of 4th Brigade, along with other comrades, went to collect dried twigs; but did not return. Therefore, Sergeant Tokim, commander of the company the Private belonged to, with his men, went searching for the lost friend.

After quite some time into their search, the Sergeant and his men were mystified to find a series of unusual shoe-prints bearing hoof-like marks (like that of a deer, to be precise) at the toe portion. But they continued searching until they began to see the same shoeprints with left and right foot impressions imprinted on the opposite directions.

Sergeant Tokim realised that their friend was gone for good; besides, they were also running short of time; for should they continue, they could miss the command. He therefore, ordered his men to withdraw. They prayed for Private Tsumongthong's soul and abandoned the search.

The python's fat

One winter day, on Tarun's bushy banks, as 2nd Lieutenant Lhousinyu Angami of 6th and his section settled down to prepare their meal, they were surprised to see their rucksacks moving, and falling from a log that they had been sitting on.

"Oh! It is a python," a soldier exclaimed. It didn't stand a chance: the whole section rushed in, killed it, and later cooked it and feasted on its meat. Yes; some Nagas were fond of snake meat. 2nd Lieutenant Lhousinyu Angami of Nerhüma village narrated how he refused to eat the meat when offered to him by his men. He also recounted how Raju Peyu Vihoshe collected the python fat, saying that it was good for healing wounds.

Laid to rest in a foreign land

On the stormy night of 11th January, 1968, Private Kivito Achumi recalls, "As we were preparing for the night's rest on a mountain, shortly after 7:30pm, comrade Khumtsa wanted to say something but his strength denied his voice; and as he rested his energy, I could see his weary eyelids closing for the last time." Soon the heavens opened up and the rain poured down as if to show that it too was mourning the death of an innocent and a loyal Naga hero. Then the thick canopies of tree branches became mere shades of dark that could not shield them from the wrath of the torrential downpour. Dripping wet from the rain, and braving the bitter winter night, the Naga Army dug the Private's grave there on a foreign mountain.

"Your commander and your comrades have indeed given their best to let you survive. Soldier dear, history shall have your name recorded as 'sacrificed at the altar of the Naga freedom movement.' Rest in peace, comrade." Captain Yeshiho, Adjutant of the command, bade the last goodbye. Raju Peyu Vihoshe, the Chaplain of the Mission prayed after reading out…

'And God shall wipe away all tears from their eyes; and there shall be no more death, neither sorrow, nor crying, neither shall there be any more pain: for the former things are passed away.' Revelation 21:4

Three shots from Corporal Nihozu's stengun marked the last respects for the Private and his mortal remains, shrouded in a traditional Sumi shawl, were laid to rest. There on a mountain corner of NgalangTaung, in an unmarked grave, another Naga soldier rests forever.

CHAPTER 4
Crossing the Border

If Nagas were brave, kind gestures of Kachin friends aided a lot to the successful undertaking of the mission. The Kachin Independence Army helped the Nagas of the Mission by providing its army as guides; providing food supplies and such other logistic supports as were within its jurisdiction. The Kachin Independence Army, led by Brigadier Zau Tu, entered into a covenant with the Naga Army.

However, once they entered Kachin land, they were hit with another little thing that had great impact: salt scarcity. There was great limitation in the rationing of salt. Quarter masters of the commands would really struggle to make an equal distribution of salt to every mess. Although there were other essential items that were very low and difficult to find, salt dominated the scarcity, because without it, the food would taste bland.

"We were forced to roast meat and fishes whenever we found it, for, to prepare a curry without salt would be as bad as not having any," expressed the veterans.

"We were also told by the KIA guides that people in some villages would take a pinch of salt and place it on the tip of a child's tongue to make the baby stop crying," continued the veterans.

Abandoned at Pinnoshu Village

On 12th January, 1968, they arrived at Pinnoshu, a Kachin village, a rather big village. Here, they rested for a night and moved the next day, but without Lance Corporal Satoi Wotsami of Ghokimi. He was left at the village due to illness.

Later, on their return journey, KIA soldiers linked him with the command, and while at Sangkhumti, a Naga Village in the Sub-Division of Kuisam, Kiphrie district, an order was given not to go out of the camp without permission; but he went out in search of food and never returned. He was killed by the village guards.

Lance Corporal Satoi Wotsami was about 30 years of age and was studying in class eight when he was conscripted into Naga Army by Lieutenant Mighishe aka Nikheto of Shesulimi. He was assigned into 23rd Coy of 14th Battalion, 5th Brigade, 2nd Division, Central Command of Naga Army, bearing Army No. 21545.

He had just got engaged to a lady from his village when he was commissioned for the mission. When he did not return from the mission, his parents, Mr. and Mrs. Sukhavi Wotsami, and family members, in his honour erected a memorial stone by the roadside of the village in 1971.

The Enchanted Forest

On the 14th of January 1969, in the heart of a dense forest, while they prepared to settle down, a strange order was given out. It prompted many Nagas to believe that the forest was an enchanted one. "Listen up, comrades; our KIA guides have advised us to avoid cutting trees, and to abstain from making much noise. They say these jungles have queer behaviour of a heavy downpour and storm at the sound and noises of a human being," skeptically announced Raju Peyu Vihoshe Shohe, the translator.

The Nagas had presumed that, in an attempt to keep the enemy from finding clues of their presence in the jungle, the KIA guides had just lied to them. They were convinced that it was an obvious lie, but they honoured it just to please them, and therefore prepared their meal in silence, with dried twigs using bare hands. However, though unknown to the Nagas, it was a popular belief to the Kachin people that in deep forests, being noisy, shouting, singing or cutting trees would cause heavy rainfall and storm.

Illness in a dense forest

Private Salumo Sheqhi sadly narrated how he begged Lieutenant Colonel Salumo Sumi, commander of the 14th at Mukalimi HQ, to spare him from the Mission. "My father was sick, so I requested the Commander to spare me from the Mission; but my request was denied: So, I left my ailing father behind and left for China along with the rest of my comrades," he said, resentfully.

One day, while in the middle of an extremely dense forest, Private Salumo Sheqhi, fell too ill to walk or even move. He gratefully recounted how his comrades helped him to survive.

"Leave me behind, you should not suffer for my sake," said I, but my comrades, especially our commander 2nd Lieutenant Yekhalu Jimo, replied that they would never leave me behind. They carried all my baggage and weapons for two days," recounted Private Salumo. "Without their support, I would have been lost or abandoned in a foreign jungle to perish," gratefully concluded the Private.

This son of Lachekhu Sheqhi of Mishilimi village was conscripted into the Naga Army by one Lieutenant from Natsumi village in the year 1965. Later, he served as bodyguard of the President of FGN, Mr. Scato Swu. Before the mission, he was attached to Lieutenant Yekhalu Jimo, 2 I/C of 24 Coy, 14th Battalion.

Towels, clothes and caps as rice-huskers

On a certain January day of 1969, grains of rice were rationed to every company and units. A stern message was given that they should use it judiciously, for the days ahead appeared tough. They were told that in the region, there would be a gap of minimum five days before they can reach any village.

Having experienced one such situation just a few days back when they had to sleep in the jungle with no signs of villages within their reach, they dug holes on the ground, placed their caps in it and using them as mortars, de-husked the rice with wooden pestles.

"We made use of everything we were carrying, spread a towel or shawl, and with plates, winnowed down the rice barn, packed it up in our bags and carried on," said Private Zuheto Chishi of 12th Battalion.

Sickness - our dreaded enemy

In the absence of proper rest, proper nutrition and getting exposed to an extremely hostile and cold winter climate, sickness was imminent, and many fell ill. Cases of three soldiers needed immediate attention.

The 4th Battalion Corporal Kahie Angami, of Viphoma village, the 6th Battalion Private Vitsomo Kense, of Tuophema village, and the 16th Battalion Private Nzanpemo Lotha, of Mekokla Village, were therefore left at Kachin Independence Army camp.

None of the three missed the command when it returned from China. However, only Corporal Kahie Angami reached home, while the other two star-crossed soldiers could not reach either of the destinations. Private Vitsomo Kense was killed in a battle at Old Tikhao village, and Private Nzanpemo Lotha was killed at Kenchung village by the Village Guards of the region.

A story within a story

For many, trudging the snowy mountains of Michikhu was a fearsome yet quite an adventurous experience. Overlooking the beautiful Hukwang valley ahead, erased the pain they endured to reach its summit. On a ramp at the summit, as they rested, Raju Peyu Vihoshe recalled his early schooling days at Aizuto Primary School and narrated a story of Evangelist Khuviqhe of Zaphumi, who used to talk about his vision.

"Nagas shall one day venture out to a big nation in the east, and in the mission many shall perish, like gourds withering and decaying, and many more shall be imprisoned." Raju Peyu Vihoshe was a little worried that their mission must have been foretold, and that it was not as appealing as they thought.

"Oh, Vihoshe, you must tell me the story again when we next get to sit," said Isak Chishi Swu.

"Sure, Sir, I ask that we continue resting, or take a step or two and rest again, to continue the story," jested Vihoshe Shohe.

"Raju Peyu Vihoshe was a happy and jolly man who would keep everyone around him happy with his jokes and kind manners," recalled the veterans.

"If General Mowu and I, or either of us, perishes in this mission, tell our people and everyone that we are alive in a foreign land, but never must you say that we are dead; for by that, shall India continue to fear the Nagas," advised Isak Chishi Swu.

Despite being menaced by the snowy route that became untraceable after every few men walk past by and the imminence of fatal fall into the dark crevasses, the Nagas trudged up and down the snowy mountain.

They were uninformed of a fresh mound at the foot of the mountain on the other side, a grave that held a victim of the snow there. Surely, at the end of the journey, beyond the snow and the mountains, lay death, impatiently awaiting their arrival.

Prayer of an American Missionary

One Sunday, at a makeshift village in the middle of the jungle, Mr. Sadow, a Salongkuba in KIA, a rank which is an equivalent of Sub-Divisional officer or Raju Peyu in the Naga parlance, guided them to the hut of a Missionary, Rev. Morse.

The man happened to be an American Christian missionary who was driven out by the Chinese communists from China for preaching the Gospel of Christ. He was pleased to meet these Naga freedom fighters.

"I have read about your struggle and have also heard of your story but never have I met any Naga Army. I am delighted to meet the Naga freedom fighters," exclaimed the missionary.

"You could have served in any big towns or cities, why have you chosen to serve in such a remote village as this?" asked a surprised Naga.

The missionary smiled and replied, "I am where God has wanted me to be, and I serve at His will not mine."

Later that day in the Sunday service, Rev. Morse exhorted the Nagas to remain close to God at all times, and be saved from harm.

"Each step you take and each sunset carries you further into a world unknown to you, further from your home and the loved ones; similarly, if you take a step away from God, you shall be drifted further off from His grace and protection. You must therefore remain closer and be with God at all times and He shall take you safe into your destinations," preached the missionary.

When it was time for them to bid goodbye, Mrs. Morse wished them well, and innocently said, "May you never suffer at the hands of communist Chinese." "Control your tongue, mummy," quickly interrupted the missionary, and continued, "May the God we serve be your guide as you move towards a nation that does not believe in the existence of God."

People of the village were mostly Christians. They were Lisu tribes of Kachin people living in Burma. Lisu tribes of Kachin are found also in the Sagaing region of Burma and in the Yunnan province of China.

The final goodbye of a Private

To avoid Burmese Forces' merciless invasions, the Kachin people often resorted to taking shelter in makeshift huts deep in the jungles or jhum fields, and the villages were often left abandoned. At one such village, Private Neisielie Angami, 6th of Kohima village, fell from a tree when he climbed a snag to collect a dead bough and the under branches for firewood. He suffered severe abdominal injury. "After few days his bladder worsened and he could no longer walk alongside the command; so, we left him at a Kachin village," recounted 2nd Lieutenant Lhousinyu Angami.

During the return trip, Private Neisielie, like others, was linked with the command; but he decided to stay back because he was convinced that his injured bladder would be a problem to the comrades.

For the last time, Neisielie bade goodbye to his comrades; and, sadly, was never heard of again.

Can a rifle swim?

One day, while fording the river Chindwin, a Private belonging to Southern Command dropped his rifle into the river. In such dreadful waters, one must have thought that it was better to have a rifle lost than a life. Nobody had dared to even tarry in that strong current, but General Mowu plunged into the waters, searched the river bed and in due time, surged up with the rifle. "I still admire and salute the General's courage," excitedly narrated Private Tusangchu Longpfürr. Tusangchu is now a Brigadier Retired and a Kilonser or Minister in the Isak-Muivah faction of the National Socialist Council of Nagalim/ Government of the People's Republic of Nagalim.

China border in sight

Kachin Independence Army was the military wing of Kachin Independence Organisation which was headed by its founder, General Zau Seng, as the President, and Brigadier Zau Tu, younger brother of General Zau Seng, as its Deputy Head in the form of Vice-President.

Brigadier Zau Tu was a lean, fair and a handsome officer besides being a brave and a great strategist. He commanded a great sense of fear and admiration from his soldiers. He belongs to Lahtaw clan of Jinghpaw tribe.

KIA soldiers were fairly convinced that the Zau brothers occupied the highest post and became their supreme leaders because of their parents' prayers and upbringing. Their parents, it is said, were a God-fearing couple, and that had laid a solid foundation for their leadership.

In the meeting with Brigadier Zau Tu, the Brigadier put forth a proposal before Isak and General Mowu. "Give us your present arms and ammunition, and bring some also from China when you return, and we shall escort you to your destinations today and tomorrow when you go back home. We will also arrange food supplies for your men, tend to the injured, and take care of any that may get de-linked from the command," proposed Brigadier Zau Tu.

The proposal to the two Naga leaders was quite acceptable. The three also agreed that the two organisations (Naga National Council / Federal Government of Nagaland and Kachin Independence Organisation / Kachin Independence Army) shall help each other in the future. The Nagas, therefore, handed over their arms, approximately more than 200 arms and a few thousands rounds to the KIA in the presence of Major Kamthui, commander of the 2nd Battalion KIA.

Brigadier Zau Tu then assigned 100 KIA soldiers who escorted them safely to the Chinese border. The command rested at the Brigade Headquarter of KIA 6th column for two days, and on 30th January, 1968, 100 soldiers of KIA escorted them out of their camp until they reached the China border. The KIA soldiers also helped them cross Malikha river on 5th February1968, using bamboo rafts.

As they neared Chinese borders, the veterans recalled, "We were so eager to see our dream land, China, that the pain and trouble we underwent had completely vanished when we arrived at the borders."

ENRC men blocked from going any further

At 2nd Brigade Headquarters of the Kachin Independence Army, Brigadier Simmon Somrah, commander of the 30 Eastern Naga Revolutionary Council soldiers, had innocently revealed their identity. The KIA authority therefore refused any further entry into its jurisdiction, because the ENRC at that time were not on good terms with the Kachin Independence Army.

Extremely disappointed by the turn of events, Private Tusangchu even confronted Isak Chishi Swu when they were told to return from the Bde HQ. "How can you just send us back when we have suffered and walked this far almost to the borders of China?" bellowed Private Tusangchu Longpfur in desperation.

"Young man, I can do nothing, for your commander has revealed that you do not belong to the Naga National Council/Federal Government of Nagaland but to the Eastern Naga Revolutionary Council of Khaplang," calmly replied Isak Chishi Swu.

After quite a commotion, Brigadier Zau Tu finally negotiated with Brigadier Simmon, commander of the ENRC, and agreed to arrange a training centre for the new recruits of the ENRC who were denied entry into China.

PHONAG training camp

The ENRC soldiers were then taken to a new camp that was established just to train the new recruits and the soldiers of ENRC. The training centre was named PHONAG which is a portmanteau word for Jingphaw and Nagas. 'PHO' stands for Jingphaw. Kachin people in their language are known as Jingphaw whereas the name Kachin was used and popularized by the Europeans. 'NAG' stands for the Nagas.

PHONAG, thus meant a training camp of Kachin people and the Nagas. At PHONAG training camp, the ENRC soldiers were imparted three months training in basic military and guerrilla warfare. By the end of the fourth month, they were sent back home with five guns and a few hundred rounds. One G-III rifle, a sten gun, pistol and two numbers of 303 rifles were gifted to those ENRC soldiers by the KIA.

Incautious Burmese Unit

On the 8th February 1968, they were guided through thick jungles before they made their way up a hill. From the top they saw an incautious Burmese Unit that they had walked past. The KIA soldiers were well informed of the terrain and the presence of Burmese forces at the Borders. They could therefore manoeuvre the Naga army into the Chinese borders.

"They must have been playing cards or some other such games; for when we walked near them, they were all seated looking down at something below. There were four to five of them. We took a detour and walked past the last men of Burmese forces straight into the safe borders of China, with the guidance of the KIA guides," recounted Captain Sanguto Chase.

Burma International Border

On the morning of 11th February 1968, the command safely reached the China–Burma International Border. Here they even gave away their extra clothing and baggage to the KIA soldiers who had safely escorted them to their destination. KIA soldiers, having accomplished their assigned mission, collected the baggage and waved their hands as they swiftly disappeared into the jungle.

Far from the enemy and free from any immediate harm, the Nagas happily settled for the night's rest there at the borders. They must have felt safe and secure, but the raging storm on the horizon that they had failed to notice, soon caught up and lashed them with a wintry storm. Next morning, they woke to a beautiful carpet of snow that had blanketed the area in freezing rain the previous night. They had not the slightest idea that their mission had vicious and impending spikes (of betrayal and death) hidden, just like those dark roots and branches that waited, hidden beneath the white slabs of ice.

While they cheerfully splatted each other with snowballs and rolled over those icy slopes, they failed to surmise the truth that they had accepted the mission, uninformed of its consequences. The mission had some horrendous experiences concealed for them, just like the snow there.

A soldier suffered an injury from one of those stuffs that was hidden below the snow.

Reception by People's Liberation Army of China

The next day, the People's Liberation Army of China arrived in trucks, prepared food for them and by afternoon, took them away to its border HQ at Kadumkai in Yunnan province. Thus, on the 13th February 1968, they set their feet on Chinese soil. There, they stayed for eight days before they were taken to their training centre at Lijiang.

It took 67 days for the command to reach China from Nagaland. Out of 312 Naga Army, only 300 actually reached China. Twelve Naga Army failed to make it to China.

Pte. Mhalevo	Drowned at Tizu River
Pte. Ghilekha, 14th Battalion.	Deserted at Chomi
Pte. Sheniyie, 14th Battalion.	Deserted at Chomi
Pte. Tsinthon Tikhir, 4th Bde Staff	Deserted at Solonokcheu
Pte. Toripkiu Thikir, 4th Bde Staff	Deserted at Solonokcheu
Corporal Tsumonthong Tikhir, 4th Bde Staff	Lost in Ngalang dense forest
Pte. Khumtsa, 14th Battalion.	Died at Ngalang mountain
Lance Corporal Satoi, 14th Battalion.	Left at Phinnoshu village
Corporal Kahie Angami, 4th Battalion.	Left at a KIA Camp
Pte. Nzanpemo Lotha, 17th Battalion.	Left at a KIA Camp
Pte. Vitsomo Kense, 6th Battalion.	Left at a KIA Camp
Pte. Neisielie Angami, 6th Battalion.	Left at a Kachin village

Thirty ENRC soldiers were also commissioned by Khaplang, but Khotsea Longpfürr was captured by Burmese forces in a fight at Solonokcheu and only 29 returned from KIA 2nd Brigade HQ.

CHAPTER 5
China Rolls Out the Red Carpet

A week and a day later, at Kadumkai border HQ of PLA in Yunnan province; military trucks arrived and convoyed the Nagas to Lijiang training centre on the 22nd February 1968.

After a month's stay, they were divided into four groups and taken on a tour. The first group was with Isak and General Mowu; the second group was led by Captain Gwovilie; the third group by Captain Kochu Pochury and the fourth group, comprising mostly Privates and NCOs could not go due to time limitation.

The 5-year promise

When Isak Chishi Swu along with General Mowu and others approached Peking, they could see the airport lit up below them. Marshal Chen Yi, Foreign Minister of the People's Republic of China, was already at the airport awaiting their arrival. The Minister received the President's Special Envoy and took them to a PLA Guest House where they stayed for over a couple of weeks.

Two days into their stay in Peking, Marshal Chen Yi, the Foreign Minister of China, invited Isak Chishi Swu for dinner and meeting at 'The Great Hall of the People' in Peking. In the meeting, the minister encouraged the President's Special Envoy and his men. "We shall help you attain liberty and you shall witness a total transformation and development of your nation within just five years," announced Marshal Chen Yi.

The Chinese will stand with you

A few days later, the Commander-In-Chief of the People's Liberation Army invited General Mowu to a dinner and meeting at the same place. He also encouraged General Mowu and the Nagas saying, "Fear not, be resolute and fight for your liberty. You have 700 Million Chinese people standing behind you."

Isak Chishi, General Mowu and Th. Muivah, General Secretary, were aware of the fact that for a communist nation to sacrifice her blood for a Christian state would require conditions that would prove unacceptable to the Nagas. General Mowu, however, asked the Chinese Commander-In-Chief, "Is China willing to shed her blood for the Nagas?"

"If you Nagas can be united and are willing, the Chinese people are ready to shed our blood for the Nagas," replied the PLA Commander-In-Chief.

General Mowu Gwizantsu, C-in-C Naga Army

Will you recognise our sovereignty?

On a March day of 1968, in his meeting with Mr. Zhou Enlai, Premier of the People's Republic of China, at the *Great Hall of the People* in Peking, Isak Swu requested the Chinese Premier to declare recognition of Nagaland as a sovereign nation. "The Federal Government of Nagaland has commissioned me as its President's Special Envoy to your great nation, to ask of you to help our country attain liberty and to declare recognition as a sovereign nation," beseeched Isak Chishi Swu.

"Certainly, the People's Republic of China will help you develop your nation within just five years once you attain liberty, but you must be patient and wait for the right time. For if we recognize your sovereignty today, the United States of America will help your adversary and before we could come to your rescue, your small nation will be crushed and you shall have suffered in vain," replied the Premier with a friendly smile that carried a bit of a sad expression. "People's Republic of China is willing to offer any other help, make it available and keep fighting for your rights until the time is right," he continued.

Mr. Zhou Enlai helped the Nagas with a huge quantity of Indian rupees and gold. The Premier was also kind enough to allow the Nagas to carry extra arms and ammunition when Isak requested that they needed some for the KIA friends as a part of their agreement.

It is assumed that had the Nagas agreed to become Communist, China was ever ready to send its army and liberate the Nagas from the clutches of Indian grip; but the three Naga leaders did not fall for it.

Isak Chishi Swu, President's Special Envoy to China

Nagas receive an aeroplane

On a sunny March day of 1968, while flying from Baoshan to Khunming, deep into the skies, clouds greeted the plane that carried another group led by Captain Kochu Pochury and Captain Gwovilie Angami with a turbulence of downdraft and buffeted it a little unpleasantly. A strong wave of high-pitched screams rushed from the lungs of the 45 petrified Naga soldiers, filled the plane and even surprised their instructors and the stewardesses as well. "When the plane jolted and swiftly descended, my heart actually began to thump like a sledgehammer," said Yekhalu, a veteran who was on the plane that day.

The hostesses with their smiling faces comforted them saying, "Meiguan xi" meaning "It is okay" and even danced just to show how safe they were from harm.

However, for the group of men, most of whom had not even taken a bicycle ride and being airborne for the first time in their lives, even a normal turbulence was an experience, embracing death herself. When they encountered turbulence just above Khunming, there again they gave a yell of fear in unison.

Later, when they landed in Peking airport, Chinese instructors who had accompanied them, pointing at the aeroplane, said, "Pengyou he tongzhimen, friends and comrades, behold your aeroplane! This is Nagas' aeroplane, it belongs to the Nagas. As long as you are here in China, the plane is yours."

Captain Kochu thanked the instructors before they were taken to the 8th floor of a PLA guest house in Peking. There again, they displayed some surprise at the lift and the well-furnished rooms that they had never seen before, not even in their most pleasant dreams.

Muivah exhorts the Naga Army

The three groups returned from their tour trips and were ready to begin political classes. Th. Muivah, the Secretary of Naga National Council, with his unfaltering energy and determination for freedom and Naga liberty, exhorted the Nagas. He even sang a song.

> *The east wind is blowing over,*
> *Over the ranges of my land,*
> *Oh my Lord, my Jehovah!*
> *What shall I do, it shall harm,*
> *It shall harm, my Lord my Jehovah!*

Th. Muivah, Gen. Secy. NNC

Muivah continued his powerful talk with a riddle.

"When stranded on a stormy bank with no vessel ahead, and the wrath of inevitable menace chases right behind, if satan appears and offers to ferry ye across, would you accept it, or refuse and suffer loss?" asked Muivah

"Today, we have come these thousand miles and are stranded on the shores of helplessness, with India right behind. Communist China has offered us help to enable us to throw out the enemy from our land. We are a Christian nation; however, we must accept the Dragon's help, for we are here not to become communists but to equip ourselves and regain our sovereignty suppressed by India," Thuingaleng Muivah cleverly exhorted the Nagas.

Idols versus the living God

The Chinese Communist Party (CCP), an atheist organisation that ruled the People's Republic of China during the time Nagas landed in China, had idolized its Chairman Mao and had likened him unto a god. People's Liberation Army soldiers were made to salute Mao Zedong's image and chant, "Mao zhuxi wan sui" meaning long live, Chairman Mao.

The Nagas had no means of escape from the act that violated their creed. They were also told to chant the line. First thing in the morning and last in the evening daily, they were made to fall in line before a huge framed image of Mao Zedong and salute it. And waving "The Little Red Book"- Quotations from Chairman Mao, they would chant "Mao Zhuxi wan sui, Mao Zhuxi wan sui, Mao Zhuxi wan sui."

However, even in the midst of people who did not believe in God, a PLA instructor, probably Christian, would secretly abstain from saluting and bowing before an idol (Chairman Mao's image). The instructor would also encourage the Nagas to abstain from the idolatrous act.

"A Chinese PLA instructor, probably a Christian, secretly gestured us to rather worship the living God in heaven and to not salute and bow before an image," explained Yekhalu Jimo.

One Sunday morning, when, as was their custom, the Nagas had gathered to worship the living God, some Chinese instructors interfered and rebuked them for worshipping God. One of them was emboldened enough to even try touching the God the Nagas were worshipping. "Where is this God of yours? We do not see it nor do we get to touch it!" mocked the instructor.

Isak Chishi stood up and humbly replied, "But you salute and worship the image of Chairman Mao, an idol of a mortal and God's created being, and we worship and serve the God that created the universe, the heavens and the earth and everything that is in it. Our God the Holy Spirit is amidst us even now." The answer quietened those instructors, and thereafter a house was arranged for the Nagas to worship their God without any interference.

China and East Pakistan training

General Mowu, Isak Chishi Chishi, and others like Tokim Tikhir, Captain Sakolie, Captain Sanguto, 2nd Lieutenant Lhousinyu, 2nd Lieutenant Zhehoto, 2nd Lieutenant Yekhalu Jimo, Lance Corporal Tokiye Wotsa and many more had also been to East Pakistan (Bangladesh) on a mission. From their earlier experiences, they could easily make out the vast differences in training offered by the two nations.

Training in East Pakistan (present-day Bangladesh) highly emphasised military basics. Handling of small firearms and ammunition, bayonet fighting, and few basics of hand and foot combat were taught. Strategies on how to execute an ambush in towns and near an enemy outpost without harming the civilians were also taught.

Training imparted by East Pakistan was effective and useful, but the Chinese training was entirely different. The communist training wholly stressed revolutionising the thoughts of these Nagas from being a mere fighter to becoming a staunch revolutionary. The training perhaps was aimed at imparting Maoism to the Naga Army.

Books on Mao Zedong's thoughts, of three volumes, were issued to any who could read and write English, stating that it shall be preserved for them in the Chinese archives. Sergeant Honivi Yeptho remembers the Chinese officials telling them, as they were handed the books, "Read it, write your names on it and we shall keep it preserved for you in the archives. Come back and get it when you attain sovereignty."

They were taught political classes, where they were made to read books on Chairman Mao's sayings and the tenets of Maoism. They were taught the National Anthem, "Dong Fang Hong-The East is Red," which was the country's National Anthem during the time. They would sing it and salute Chairman Mao's image every morning.

Political classes were conducted, with instructors speaking English, Hindi, Assamese and Burmese, and they were divided accordingly.

On Sundays, only two meals were served saying that a soldier should not eat on days they do not work, whereas on other days three meals were provided. A very strict routine was followed:

04:30 Arise
06.00 Exercise
07.00 Breakfast
08.00 – 12.00 Class
12.00 – 13.00 Lunch
13.00 – 14.00 Rest
14.00 – 15.00 Discussion
15.00 – 17.00 Games and Sports
17.00 – 16.00 Dinner/ Supper
17.00 – 22.00 Study
22.00 – Sleep

Those who disobeyed were punished.

Though Maoism dominated the training, some of the Chairman Mao's basic tactics of guerrilla warfare were also taught in those classes.

Sparrow warfare: "The enemy advances, we retreat; the enemy camps, we harass; the enemy tires, we attack; the enemy retreats, we pursue." (Chairman Mao.)

It is warfare where a few soldiers attack the enemy at different places but at a constant pace or in a planned manner. In it, the revolutionists intentionally take only one or two at a time and the next attempt is done at a very far place so the enemy does not take it too seriously, but it hampers the economy of the enemy nation.

"When you go home, apply it, and in thirty days, India will have thirty fallen soldiers. It will weigh down her economy and you shall gradually have her overthrown from your country," advised the instructors.

Tunnel warfare was also taught. The Chinese PLA also indoctrinated the Nagas with one of Mao's popular quotations, *"Political power grows out of the barrel of a gun."* The effect of this continues to this day.

"Liberty can never be attained without bloodshed. Never enter into a peace talk with the oppressor; but should you for some unavoidable circumstances do so, never stop firing, for the moment the guns stop firing, your freedom is silenced," cautioned the Chinese instructors.

Discipline: Discipline is one of the many qualities where the PLA outshines most armies of the world. They were taught to follow discipline at any cost. An army should never destroy public crops and property, even during a mission. If they chanced to do it, the same should be repaid or compensated by those responsible.

One day Corporal Vizotuo, of Kohima village, belonging to 6th Battalion and 2nd Lieutenant Lhousinyu were sent to fetch rations for the camp, along with other Chinese drivers. Corporal Vizotuo's vehicle hit a cow, ran over its hoof and injured the animal. "We were soon surrounded by the Chinese civilians, who would not let us pass without being compensated. It was only after some PLA officers intervened that we were allowed to pass," recounted 2nd Lieutenant Lhousinyu Angami.

Not all were given political classes, but some were taken to Baoshan and given driving classes while some were given medical training at different hospitals in Baoshan.

Is there a God?

One day, during Naga Army Officers' platoon discussion at Lijiang training centre, a Chinese instructor asked the group to point out if they had observed any shortcomings in the conduct of PLA and the Communist party, and suggestions, if any. Most of the officers chose to keep quiet, with the exception of 2nd Lieutenant Zhehoto Awomi, who gave a brave comment with the help of Vihoshe, who translated his message to the Chinese instructor.

He said, "Nagaland is a Christian state where societies have been stratified into the haves and the have-nots; it is a nation that believes in Christ and God without any sign of equality amongst its citizens. I marvel at the fact that yours is a community where everyone is equal and has a society ruled by peace and harmony.

"If only you believe also in the existence of God and His love, Chinese people could be the only people on earth that will receive salvation. The only and the biggest flaw I find in you is your belief in the non-existence of God," continued 2nd Lieutenant Zhehoto.

"Hao, good," said the instructor to the Lieutenant giving a thumbs up.

The Chinese instructor, however, argued with the translator, saying that the communists were right in believing in the non-existence of God, and that the Nagas were worshipping and believing in the existence and powers of God in vain.

Vihoshe rebutted the instructor with a Chinese story of an old foolish man whose hard work and perseverance in removing a pair of the mountains before his house earned God's favour; that the gods fulfilled his dreams. He continued, "If you do not believe in God, why would Chairman Mao refer to this story in some of his speeches? Also, why did he say that through hard work and perseverance, the Chinese Communist Party could win the heart of God?"

"It is because of the fear and respect we have for Chairman Mao that we say so; but my father still offers home prayer with us," replied the instructor.

London awaits

Isak wanted to go to London to meet A. Z. Phizo, but the Chinese authorities responded that he had to wait for three months before he can fly to London. He felt that three months would be too long a wait, so he began dry fasting and grew exceptionally weak in just a week's time. "Tell me, what is ailing you that you should stop eating. I find nothing wrong with your health," inquired the Chinese lady doctor who examined Isak.

"I must fly down to Dhaka to meet my comrades and to London and I want it quickly. I am therefore fasting and praying for God's intervention," replied Isak.

"Why have you hurt yourself just for this?" replied the astounded doctor.

The Chinese authorities made necessary arrangements and helped Isak and his Personal Secretary, K. Shikhu fly down to Dhaka, East Pakistan (present day Bangladesh). There, he met General Ayub Khan, left his PS and flew to Karachi, Pakistan, en route to London.

At a hotel in London, Mr. Isak and the President NNC, Mr. A.Z. Phizo had a marathon discussion which lasted for six days and six nights. All necessary information and documents that he had carried from Nagaland were presented to the President. A.Z Phizo also sent a letter to General Mowu Gwizantsu who was in China.

Bizarre flood

One June day of 1968, waters in the river Lijiang overflowed and submerged a part of the camp.

It is Mother Nature's way that fishes should flow with and in the waters. However, the day witnessed a bizarre flood of fishes that swarmed into the camp. Naga Army men happily collected them and prepared delicious dishes.

"Lieutenant Sir, we have prepared it well for the officers, please dine with us," asked Corporal Nihozu of 11th Battalion. "I remember an old saying, that an unnatural way of getting meat aplenty is an ill omen; a harbinger of a danger," replied Second Lieutenant Yekhalu Jimo and declined the dish.

The kiss of life

One summer afternoon during break hour when all the comrades were in the camp, Thongthong Tikhir of Shamator, a Private belonging to 4th Brigade Staff with a Pochury guy, another Private from 10th Battalion, jumped into Lijiang river, to cool themselves off. A Chinese guard warned them of the strong undercurrent and stopped them but they ignored the advice; and, as they enjoyed the cool waters, the Pochury guy was washed away. Thongthong quickly pulled him to safety but could not save himself from the vortex of water that carried him down the river bed.

The Chinese guard whistled the alarm and, having removed his uniform, dived into the river. In the meantime, Nagas had also rushed to the spot.

"Men, get into the water quickly and save your comrade," screamed Captain Kochu Pochury. Sergeant Chepong Pochury of 10th Battalion, aided by Private Vighozu, and a Chinese soldier rescued the Private from the jaws of death. Mouth-to-mouth resuscitation and other first aid emergency measures were initiated before he was taken to Baoshan hospital to prevent any possible complications.

Thongthong Tikhir at present is in the village as a village chief, and continues to serve the nation as Razhu Peyu in the Civil Wing of NSCN (Isak Muivah).

Here lies a Naga Hero

As a part of training, the Naga Army cultivated a paddy field in the early part of June 1968. They engaged one whole week transplanting rice seedlings. However, they could not harvest the field because they had to hurry back home before the harvest time, which was expected in the latter part of October and in the month of November.

Having laboured for a week, most Nagas felt weak and tired. One June day in 1968, there was a little drizzle, so everyone was resting at the camp; but Private Thongthong Tikhir of Chikipongru went out strolling towards the river to watch the rainbow that was hitting the bank of the river Lijiang.

"He returned dumb and would even try to run away from us. He could only show us through signs that his whole body was aching," recounted the Private's comrades.

Thongthong's illness displayed strange and bedeviled symptoms of running away from comrades; he would isolate himself, and even attempted suicide. His health deteriorated within just a day of the fever. The Chinese army then took him to Baoshan hospital; but brought him back dead three days later on 15th June 1968.

Private Thongthong was laid to rest at Lijiang Training Camp with an epitaph that read, 'Here lies a Naga Hero, Private Thongthong Tikhir of Chikipongru, 4th Bde staff, Central Command, 2nd Division, Naga Army.'

Fight between comrades

One summer afternoon, while having tea after a brief parade session, Private Pheluolou Chase of 6th cheerfully played a prank on his comrades by sprinkling a cup of water upon them. The prank did not go down well with one of the comrades. Private Maiphai Tangkhul of 7th who was most affected, lost his patience and started a fight with Private Pheluolou. The two Privates, both from the Southern Command, got into a fight before the officers resting at the Group 'A' Officers' Platoon Mess rushed down and stopped it.

The brawl between the two Privates grew into trouble by evening, when Private Pheluolou and few of his friends battered the other Private back in the camp. It almost turned into a tribal issue between the two Naga brothers on a mission in a foreign land. The news instantly reached the command authority. "Why are you being so silent about it, General? If you do not take immediate action I shall have it recorded in the national book as a national crime," said Th. Muivah to General Mowu Gwizan.

"Do not worry Sir, it shall be dealt with promptly, for I shall entrust the command Adjutant to take care of the matter," replied the General, and called for Captain Yeshiho.

"May I come in, Sir?" "Come in," says the General.

"Listen, Captain; the fight today between the two brothers has taken an ugly turn, so that it now requires our strict intervention. I want you to tackle it. Beat them or punish them, but just make sure they do not repeat it," sternly ordered the General. "Yes, Sir, I shall," said the Captain, and walked out the General's room.

Captain Yeshiho immediately ordered his men to bring before him the two Privates and those involved in the incident. When all the parties concerned had arrived, the Captain intently looked into the eyes of each of the men and began speaking.

"You with your silly behaviour have tarnished the good image of the Nagas, here in a foreign land, and the authority has viewed it with all seriousness. You deserve the severest of punishment; but since we are in a foreign land, you shall be excused of the punishment this time. But remember, if you repeat it: one step into the jungle beyond the borders you shall be shot down and shall never see our home again." The Captain then made them sign a bond in the presence of the two leaders and dismissed the men.

Barely three days after the incident, two men from the Central Command engaged in a fight. Private Nizheto Sumi of 11th and

Corporal Yehoto Sumi of 12th Battalions, while playing basketball, had a fight and punched each other hard. The Chinese soldiers tried to stop them, but the two would not listen to them. They stopped only when they heard their Captain's voice.

"Hey, you! Stop the fight immediately and stand still, that's an order," fumed Captain Yeshiho Awomi. The two soldiers, with noses bleeding, respectfully stood in attention as the Captain thrashed them with a stick.

"You are being trained not to fight each other, but the enemy. You must therefore put a stop to these foolish acts. Do not ever let me see or hear of it," warned the Captain as he beat them with three strokes each. He then ordered the two to shake each others' hand, and dismissed them.

Later in the evening, when the two were seen eating and sharing from the same plate, PLA soldiers would appreciate the Naga Army for their respect to seniors, and their heart to forgive each other.

Assassination takes place

On the 4th August 1968, a Chinese instructor rushed in and announced, "Your brave leader General Kaito Sukhai has been assassinated. He was shot at Kohima yesterday and has succumbed to it today."

Many did not believe the instructor; some even argued that the General could never be assassinated. However, there was one man among them (and perhaps a few) who knew that the General was being pursued even before they had marched out for China.

By 17th June 1967, General Kaito Sukhai had formed an Army Government and the FGN leaders viewed it as a grave threat to both its organisation and the Naga National movement. It is said that the General derived this idea of forming an Army Government from his foreign friend General Ayub Khan of East Pakistan, with whom he had good relations.

It is assumed that the infamous removal of General Kaito from C-in-C to accommodate a young and much junior officer, who had to leapfrog at least four senior and competent officers, namely Lieutenant General Dusoi, Lieutenant General Makhen, Lieutenant General Zuheto Swu and a few other Senior Major Generals, to occupy the post, had prompted the General to break away from NNC/FGN and form his own government. Perhaps that cost his life too.

General Kaito Sukhai, a brave General and one of the pioneers of the Naga National Movement was a great military strategist whose reputation instilled fear and respect even among his adversaries. He was also befittingly accredited by BBC as 'The Youngest General in the World'. The General, who was also popularly known even in some western and neighbouring countries, felt humiliated and dishonoured of his sacrifices and contributions for the nation when he was unceremoniously removed from the post of C-In-C in his absence and reassigned, from a great warrior and strategist, to a Kilonser - Minister of Defence in Civil Wing.

The General during this time was at Kuhubo camp at Shera in Leyshi Township of Sagaing region in Myanmar. He was known to the Chinese too. A Chinese instructor even told the Naga trainees that he had heard of the General's bravery and excellent war strategies and how he and his comrades had expected to meet him; for they had anticipated his being in the Mission.

Chinese undercover spies in Nagaland

The People's Liberation Army of China also deployed its soldiers as undercover spies at some strategic places in Nagaland. During discussion hour in one political class, an espionage agent who had just returned from Nagaland recounted his experiences at Zunheboto to Sergeant Honivi Yeptho and friends. "I operated at Zunheboto for two months disguised as a Nepali cobbler," asserted the man. No wonder, the Chinese even prepared Axone dishes for the Sumis saying, "You Sumis are fond of Axone." The man spoke good Hindi and a little bit of Nagamese, a lingua franca of Nagaland. That helped him remain unsuspected.

Special and advanced training by Chinese authorities

When Isak Chishi Swu returned from London, Chinese officials briefed him of the situation in Nagaland and cautioned him from heading back home at such a time. The Chinese strongly forewarned that his reception at home would be disastrous and that the mission would be made futile. China even offered for Isak and his men to stay back for at least three more years and receive special and advanced training which would include modern and sophisticated weapons. Mr. Isak Chishi Swu humbly refused the proposal and resolutely replied, "I must hurry back home and rectify the wrong. I must save my Nation from crumbling to death."

"Men, we must get ready to go home and save our house from falling into the enemy's pit," Isak ordered his men. Had they stayed back, the history of the Naga National Movement would have been scripted differently from that we read today. Mr Isak Chishi Swu was perhaps given a condition that was totally unacceptable to his faith, to the Nagas and to a Christian nation.

Isak was hell-bent on rushing back to Nagaland, despite the odds that stood against his favour. That certainly was one of the other reasons that foreshortened their training in China.

Practising for the long-haul home

Therefore, when the sixth month of political classes had ended at Lijiang training centre, they were shifted to Thungchung training centre. After target shooting and firearms training was completed, they were engaged with trail march in the jungles.

The Nagas, in full military gear and baggage, marched the jungles for over four miles on the first day, six miles the second day, ten miles the third day and fifteen to twenty miles on the fourth day. The Chinese prepared the Nagas well to carry heavy baggage before they were sent off.

The Chinese instructors were extremely pleased at the performance of the Naga Army, who displayed excellence in all types of arms in which they were trained. The Sub-Machine Gunners, M21 Semi-automatic Riflemen, Rocket-launcher Gunners, mine bomb squads, 60 MM squads, wireless operators, compass units, First Aid team; all performed so excellently that the instructors happily encouraged them.

"If you fight the enemy back home at this pace and ability, you shall soon have the enemy thrown out of your land," exclaimed the instructors. "We are also excited that Chairman Mao, on seeing your progress and smartness, will be pleased at our works and we shall receive praises from him," continued the instructors.

The Nagas, with the love for guns running in their blood, quickly learnt all the new weapons and hit the bull's eye during the target session. Most Nagas have marksmanship ability.

Armed and ready to march back

The Naga Army were armed to the teeth. Burmese forces or even the now mighty Indian Army were not as heavily equipped as the Nagas were then. They were armed with full combat kits and gear, and modern firearms with many thousands of rounds. A fully prepared Naga Army's load would weigh over thirty kilos, it is said. They were equipped with weapons like AK type 56 (also known as M22) Chinese sub-machine guns, LMGs, M21 Chinese semi-automatic rifles, RPGs, 60 MM mortars, Vereylight, compass; plus binoculars for the unit's commanders and 9 mm pistols for the officers.

AK bullet cases containing 300 and 500 rounds were carried by every soldier according to their physical fitness. The Central Command alone carried over 90 AKs, 5 LMGs, 54 M21 semi-automatic rifles, 14 9mm Pistols besides RPG, 60 mm mortars, two numbers of military radios (wireless sets), Vereylight, compass and binoculars. The same number of equipment (except the AKs, M21, and 9 mm pistols) was carried also by the Armies of Southern Command.

The President's Envoy himself carried a semi-automatic rifle with 50 rounds and a 9 mm Pistol with 20 rounds.

There were RPG and 60 mm mortar, one each for the Central and Southern Commands, and four military radios (wireless sets two each for the two commands.) As for the Central Command, one for the 4th Bde was carried by Corporal Vitoshe and one for the 5th Bde was carried by Private Piwoto Ighanumi and RPG by Private Piwoto Ghokimi both of 14th and 60 mm was carried by Corporal Kichotsing Sangtam of 11th Battalion.

Some were assigned to carry extra arms for their KIA comrades, while those who carried 300-round boxes even carried cash of ₹100,000, one lakh (hundred thousand) rupees; Captain Sanguto, Captain Gwovile, Captain Yeshiho; Lieutenant K. Shikhu carried perhaps even more than a lakh for he was the PS to the President's Special Envoy and many more. Those who carried boxes of 500 rounds, like Captain Sakolie Yokha, Second Lieutenant Zhehoto Awomi, Lieutenant Megosazo, Second Lieutenant Yekahlu Jimo, were not given even a rupee to carry.

The Communist government of China helped the Christian Naga Army with a massive amount of three million Rupees and 5 kilograms of gold.

On the evening of 18th October 1968, there at the training centre, the Nagas were given a sad farewell by the soldiers and the officers of the People's Liberation Army of China. The Chinese Government officials who attended the programme encouraged the Naga Army to be resolute and united in their fight for liberty; and further encouraged them by saying seven hundred million Chinese people were behind them. Nagas, therefore must fearlessly fight for their rights and freedom.

Farewell at the borders

On the morning of 19th October, their instructors bade them a tearful farewell before they were driven off to a village in the border areas, in 35 Chinese PLA military trucks. The next day, they began walking with Chinese PLA escorting them to the border, where the final goodbye was done.

The Chinese soldiers stood in a line, shook hands with the Naga Army soldiers and sadly said, "Phangyu he Tongzhimen tsaijien" meaning, "Friends and comrades, see you again." In some Chinese soldiers, emotions ran quite high; they would cry and wipe their tears as they shook hands.

The soldiers and instructors back in the training camp must have cried because they knew of the enemy and the troubles that the Nagas would face before they reached home; and they were apprehensive that many might perish on the way. However, not many Nagas were moved by those tears; it was to them idle tears, as they were rather happy to be finally going home. Seeing someone cry over the departure for their home made it more ridiculous to some unmindful Nagas.

"How can it be so easy for a soldier to cry? Isn't it silly for a man to shed tears easily? We're going home and I am surprised to see them cry over it!" Lieutenant Yekhalu murmured to his comrades as they innocently chuckled with no emotions at all. Meanwhile Nizheto, a Corporal from 11th Battalion, bravely said that they would fiercely fight the enemy should they come their way when a Chinese soldier suggested that there might be the presence of enemy soldiers all through their way home.

The Chinese Army officials also said that the route was the shortest and would take them just a week to be home. However, due to the presence and constant attack of the enemy, the command had to reroute; which would cost them six months and many lives to reach home.

CHAPTER 6

A Bridge Too Far

By the 22nd of October they had already set their feet on Burma land. When the sun had begun to go down, soldiers leading the advance guard on that particular leg encountered two Burmese spy soldiers equipped with rifles and spying on them. Private Akhalu of 14th Battalion said that the two had perhaps also seen the Chinese PLA forces that had come to the borders.

Instead of taking the target down, the men tried to catch them alive and even sent a message to the command authorities to advise whether to shoot or capture them alive. However, the enemy fled the scene even before they could finalise their plan of action.

Considering the massive impact the incident left upon the command, the guards had made a serious blunder in letting the two spies escape without a single shot being fired. The spies escaped and the Nagas became trapped in trouble.

Later, with the sun long gone beyond the horizon and with no signs of any villages nearby, the Nagas stopped the march and slept there in the jungle.

Failing to connect

The next day, while the sun was still young, they arrived at another Kachin village. "Wireless operators, connect me to the radios at home," called out the command adjutant Captain Yeshiho Awomi.

The two wireless operators did everything they could but failed to get any connection to the radios at home. However, they could connect to the radios back in China. It sure must have been a great joy, but the talk with the Chinese comrades, however pleasant it may have been, could not quench their thirst to hear their comrades and officers back home; so they kept trying to connect to the radios back home. On the other hand, wireless operators never knew that they were flogging a dead horse in doing so.

The Revolutionary Government of Nagaland had already stocked all the arms and ammunition along with the radio sets brought from East Pakistan at its Lita HQ of 13th and heavily guarded by the soldiers of RGN.

Abandoned outpost

They were taken aback to find an abandoned outpost of the Burmese Armed Forces at a Kachin village not far from the border area. "People in the village told us that the Burmese Forces, fearing the Chinese Army beat a hasty retreat, leaving the outpost that morning of October 25, 1968," recounted the Veterans

There are two probable theories behind the enemy forces abandoning the outpost. One, they left the outpost without attacking the Naga Army due to the propaganda spread by the two Burmese spy soldiers and the rumours that Chinese PLA soldiers were escorting the Naga Army to its borders in Nagaland. The second theory, which also corresponds to the findings of the security strategic assessment, is that Burma had planned to annihilate the Nagas deep within its territory and terrain, where there will be barely enough room for cover or return, because of the fear that the Nagas would go back to China if they had launched the attack from the border areas itself.

Burma wanted to punish the Naga Army for trespassing on its territory. It also wanted to avoid being in the black book of India; therefore, it brutally fought the Nagas to prevent them from reaching their home land.

However, what Burma utterly failed to realise was that the Nagas would never have retreated back to China, even if they were attacked right from the borders. The Nagas are fierce fighters, warriors by blood. Moreover, and most notably, they were marching back home to their loved ones. They wanted to see and to be with their families again; to be home in the land they were fighting to liberate; the land they so adore. Perhaps unknown to them, they were returning to the land that also would hold their betrayers.

I was so scared that I even cried

On the morning of 30th October, 1968, at around 8:30, they came across a deep gorge with no other way out but an old ruined rope bridge. The hanging bridge had been left abandoned for so many years that all the wooden planks had completely vanished, leaving the bridge with just the ropes that hung slack above the dark and deep blue waters.

As they approached the edge, the command leaders realised that it was practically impossible to track down into that deep gorge; it would be suicide to lead the men into such a rough and jagged cliff and to try fording the swift waters.

"Both our leaders, Isak Chishi Swu and General Mowu Gwizantsu, were completely brought to a standstill. They were both deeply troubled," Sergeant Honivi Yeptho remembered. "Isak had even fallen to his knees and begun praying. I saw Lieutenant Yekhalu Jimo and Lieutenant Megosazo Angami had already begun mending the rope bridge with bedding ropes," continued Sergeant Honivi Yeptho. However, the 80 to 100 feet length of hanging bridge proved a great undertaking for the hands of just two men.

They were soon joined by other comrades. The Nagas cautiously walked over the sagging bridge. It was feared that the old and corroded ropes would not hold the weight of soldiers in full and heavy gear, so they crossed it in threes, with the second man stepping in only when the first man had moved into the middle, so as to bring balance to the saggy ropes.

Despite being brave as a lion in the battlefields, the soldiers trudged the iron ropes as slow as a snail, so that it cost the Nagas a whole day to cross the bridge. It was already seven in the evening and darkness had long hovered in by the time the last man set his foot on the other side of the river.

2nd Lieutenant Lhousinyu Angami remembered, "After 2nd Lieutenant Yekhalu Jimo and Lieutenant Megosazo had initiated the mending, we all joined and began crossing the bridge. In the middle of the bridge the two upper ropes of the bridge would clinch at our abdomen and in the process, a few of my Southern Command comrades even lost their grenades in the waters.

"The thought of walking over that rope bridge made me so scared that I even cried. However, Lieutenant Megosazo gave me a pep talk so that I could muster courage to cross that scary bridge," recounted Private Soleo Angami, 6th Battalion of Gariphema village, with gratitude.

"You may shoot me here but never shall I cross this bridge," cried a petrified Sergeant Major. Others managed to convince him; but when a portion of rope broke away as he staggered through, the man screamed in fear, "My heart has broken, comrades!"

2nd Lieutenant Lhousinyu cheerfully described the aftermath: "Later, during leisure times in jail, when we would tease him, the Sergeant Major would happily join in our laughter"

The Naga Navy

Private Zuheto Chishi recalls, "It was on the 18th November 1968, when we stumbled upon the N'Mai Hka river. The water was too deep to wade through and it was impossible to swim across the river carrying heavy gear. The Pochury comrades whom we had nicknamed 'The Naga Navy' helped us cross the river."

The Pochury men, who belonged to 10th Battalion of 4th Brigade, 2nd Division of Central Command Naga Army, quickly prepared a bamboo raft. They engineered their experience into that makeshift raft by replacing the oars with ropes which they tied at the two ends of the raft. Some of the men swam across the river with the rope that was tied at the other end of the raft and then raft-ferried all the comrades of Central Command.

The Pochury soldiers were exceptionally good in waters and had saved many lives during and even before the Mission, back home. Therefore, they were given the nickname 'The Naga Navy,' from their comrades back home and those in the Mission.

Private Zuheto Chishi, with large tears welled up at the inner corners of his wearied eyes, recounted how he and his two friends, Private Tokiho Sumi of Nihoshe village and Private Hekiye Sumi of Vedami village, both belonging to the 12th Battalion, were saved from the mouth of death at the river the day the raft which was ferrying them tipped off and plunged them into the waters. "It was God Himself who held our hands steadfast to the raft. If not, all three of us would have been sleeping in the unmarked bed of the river N'Mai Hka," said the Private.

River N'Mai Hka takes a Naga

Meanwhile, soldiers of Southern Command were also crossing the river a little upstream at a point where the water was deeper than that of the Central Command's point. When everyone had crossed, Private Rüyahulie aka Yahu who was the last to reach the bank, was left unattended. The last section had actually forgotten to keep holding the rope and as the Private lifted his foot to step out, the raft shifted back. The waters immediately opened its dark doors and locked the Private into its suffocating world; a world far away from his comrades and loved ones. His comrades tried to retrieve him, but the water was too deep for them to dive in. "A full-length bamboo would not reach the bottom of the river." said Sergeant Honivi.

Once again, a hero from the Southern Command became the first victim during the journey back home, and the second victim of water. The bed of the river N'Mai Hka yet again became a resting place for a Naga hero, deep and far away from his loved ones and his people.

It would have then been quite a task for anybody to convince the mission men that water is a sustainer of life. To them, water, the sustainer of life, was but a cruel depriver of life; for they witnessed death from water at the beginning of their journey, back and forth.

That night they slept in a field on the other side of the river and resumed their march the next day.

CHAPTER 7

Who Will Make It Home?

By 19th November, 1968, the command had already reached Nchunglova Yang, a Kachin village between two dark and cold rivers, the N'Mai Hka and the Mali-hka. It was a small hillside village with old trenches running around the village, which had been dug by the Allied Forces during the Second World War.

Foreign Secretary and the General

The next day, Isak Chishi Swu, and General Mowu, with 50 personnel left the village for the GHQ (General Headquarters) of the Kachin Independence Army (KIA). They wanted to give Brigadier Zau Tu and the KIA leaders the arms and ammunition they had carried for them. The sight of brand-new sub-machine guns, semi-automatic rifles and a huge cache of shots might have sent Brigadier Zau Tu into ecstasy; but his moment of excitement and happiness soon switched to poignancy, as he learnt that one of his soldiers had died in a Burmese ambush of the column. The deceased was one of those soldiers who were sent to guide the column safely into the KIA GHQ.

Naga Army prepares for an ambush

Back in the village, the Naga Army, relying on their military strategic assessment and the information received from a village that they had walked past beyond the river N'Mai Hka, were prepared and expecting adversary anytime. As a matter of fact, they were rather keen to squeeze the triggers of their Chinese automatic machine guns against the enemy. The Nagas also had a desire to test-fire in auto mode, the arms they had been carrying for the last month from China. Therefore, when they learnt of the tracking down of an enemy behind them, they gladly secured the perimeter and excitedly waited for the enemy, little aware of the fate that awaited them with a cruel blow.

The 21st night of November, 1968, shortly after they had fallen asleep; Lance Corporal Kiyeto Sema experienced a disturbing dream that jolted him into a nagging wakefulness. "A heavy enemy pursuit chased us down to the edge of a catastrophic landslide that flooded down a deep gorge. Other comrades who ran into it were soon engulfed in the debris of the landslide and were all carried down the bottom of the gorge, whereas I somehow managed to jump out to safety. Just then I woke up, sweating profusely," recounted Lance Corporal Kiyeto Sema.

"Friends, I had a strange dream last night," he said to his Battalion comrades. "Please do not speak to us of your dreams, we do not wish to hear it. Every dream of yours has always been a bad one and we fear that this one would be no different," cried the Lance Corporal's Battalion mates as they ran away from him.

After a while, when every Battalion and its sections had settled down for the morning meal, the men from second Lieutenant Yekhalu's mess offered him an extra meat- a chicken head piece. It was the custom of the Nagas to offer the head piece of any meat to the eldest or the most senior, as a sign of respect, and also because the custom forbids the young to have the head before the elders or seniors. However, for some unknown reason, the Lieutenant decided to give away his share of meat to someone else.

"I do not know why, but I felt the need to let anybody have it but myself; and as I scanned for whom I should give it to, Corporal N-Nungrhomo immediately caught my attention. I noticed his unusually sorrowful countenance, so I decided that it was going into the Corporal's plate," said second Lieutenant Yekhalu.

Let firing commence

On the 22nd November 1968, the Central Command that was left at the village as rear-guard, dispatched its Battalions to their relevant positions. In the north, on the upper road of the village that connected the road to N'Mai Hka river to Mali-hka river and the way to KIA GHQ, the 10th took hold of the position as the rear-guard. The 11th was placed behind them in the village as rear-guard support, 12th in the middle of the village as rear-guard reserve and 14th in the north-eastern part of the village where enemy assault was anticipated. The Southern Command, taking the approach road below the village, had moved towards the river Mali-hka as advance guard and leaving the village a bit behind. At 10:30 a.m., whizzing bullets silenced the sweet chants of the blowing wind and the reverberating sounds of the river that flowed below the village.

Will you take care of my son?

As firing began, Sergeant Major Chükhüra Pochury of 10th who was commanding the duty, was shot down with mortal head injury. Corporal Chipung Pochury and Corporal Kharutsu Pochury of 10th Battalion, under the shield of RPGs, hand grenades and covering fire of M22 sub-machine guns of Corporal Zuheto Lukhami and his fellow comrades of 11th Battalion, bravely retrieved the wounded comrade and handed him over to 2nd Lieutenant Zhehoto Awomi.

The 2nd Lieutenant and his men shaved and dressed the wounded head, applied some Chinese medicine and bandaged it; but the Sergeant could not fight back to life. In the hands of the 2nd Lieutenant Zhehoto, Sergeant Major Chükhüra uttered his last words. "I have laid down my life for the Naga nation; please tell the government to take care of my only son back home," choked the Sergeant.

The 2nd Lieutenant Zhehoto and his men buried the fallen Sergeant in a cabin hut of an old abandoned field. The fight for the liberty of the Nagas and her sovereignty once again leaves a Naga wife widowed and her children orphaned.

It is painful that those heroes have been left unsung to this day and those family members of the lost ones are still uncompensated. What makes it more disheartening and disgusting is the fact that they will perhaps remain unsung and their families uncompensated forever.

Death is only a breath away

Meanwhile on a hillside, few yards below a deserted lone house, 2nd Lieutenant Yekhalu Jimo, Corporal N-Nungrhomo Lotha of 16th Battalion, Lance Corporal Kiyeto of 12th Battalion and Private Akhalu of 14th Battalion had positioned themselves on a half-dug mound that served a natural defence. "There can be no better spot than this one to shield ourselves and also to attack the enemy. Friends, never abandon this shield for another place," 2nd Lieutenant Yekhalu instructed his three comrades.

Just then he saw N-Nungrhomo moving out. "Corporal, do not go out there, that defence is too shallow, get back!" "Ei saab ami mota ase, bhoi nalage- Sir, I am a man, I am not afraid," bravely replied Corporal N-Nungrhomo, and fearlessly leaped forward into a decrepit and shallow fire trench (that had been dug by the Allied forces during the Second World War) in an open space and crouched down in the defence.

In a little while a host of Burmese soldiers showed up on a hilltop beneath pipal trees, looking down towards them and began creating a commotion. The four released their unforgiving rain of bullets into the crowd of enemy soldiers and shot down many of them. However, Coporal N-Nungrhomo, who stood exposed to the Burmese soldiers, could not hide himself from the deadly touch of the enemies' bullets that shot into his defenceless trench.

Lance Corporal Kiyeto Sema suffered injury and had to leave, while Private Akhalu also abandoned the spot.

Meanwhile 2nd Lieutenant Yekhalu continued firing, almost emptying the third magazine of his type 56 Chinese AK, and soon realised that his other comrades had left him alone. By the time he turned towards

N-Nungrhomo, he saw the Corporal still crouched in the defence, clinging on to his AK rifle as if still ready to fire but the head was lowered and resting on the edge of that fire trench, down, never to be lifted. And as he looked at the lifeless body, he recalled the morning mealtime-incident.

"Corporal, take this and eat it." "Thank you, Sir, but I cannot, for how am I supposed to eat something meant for seniors?" "Oh, Corporal, put it back onto your plate and just eat it."

"Sir, I feel unworthy of it." "Listen, N-Nungrhomo, there are many of you here but I have chosen you, so have it and cheer up, we never know when we shall next get to have such a delicious thing as this."

"Ok then, I shall eat it, Sir, thank you."

The Lieutenant tried to recover the body of the fallen comrade, but it proved impossible to do the job single-handedly, especially when he was without any covering fire. "The only way I could retrieve the fallen comrade's body was to move up his trench and expose myself to the enemy; and to do that without any covering fire would have been suicide," sadly recounted the Lieutenant.

For one last time, he looked at the fallen comrade and sadly bade him goodbye. "Soldiers we are, and if not today, tomorrow still we all may die. Lucky are those who shall have people to tell their stories, their sacrifices and their bravery. I shall surely recommend your name to our government when I reach home, rest in peace, comrade N-Nungrhomo." A foreign corner once again became a resting place for a Naga hero.

Showers of bullets forced the Lieutenant to retreat; and as he ran for cover, he tripped and fell down. When the enemy, presuming him dead, held their fire for a while, the Lieutenant rose again and jumped into a shallow runnel that zigzagged down to the south of the village. But as he ran from one direction to another a bullet nearly killed him, and injured his forehead.

By the time he reached his friends, the column had already decamped towards the river beyond the village. "Is anyone behind, Sir?" inquired the men in position. "No," shouted back the Lieutenant; "N-Nungrhomo is dead. How about Private Akhalu and Lance Corporal Kiyeto, have they come with you?" asked the Lieutenant.

"Private Akhalu has retreated while Lance Corporal Kiyeto sustained severe injury and has been evacuated to a safer place," replied the men. "Go join the men down at the camp, Sir."

Recovery is not an option

While fighting alongside 2nd Lieutenant Yekhalu Jimo, Lance Corporal Kiyeto shot down at least two enemy soldiers, but when he got injured he left the position with Private Akhalu, and was evacuated to a nearby Kachin village.

Lance Corporal Kiyeto suffered fracture of rib, and injury to liver. Lieutenant Dr. Samson Luikham, the Chief Medical Officer of Naga Army, who examined the injured, recommended six months of complete rest.

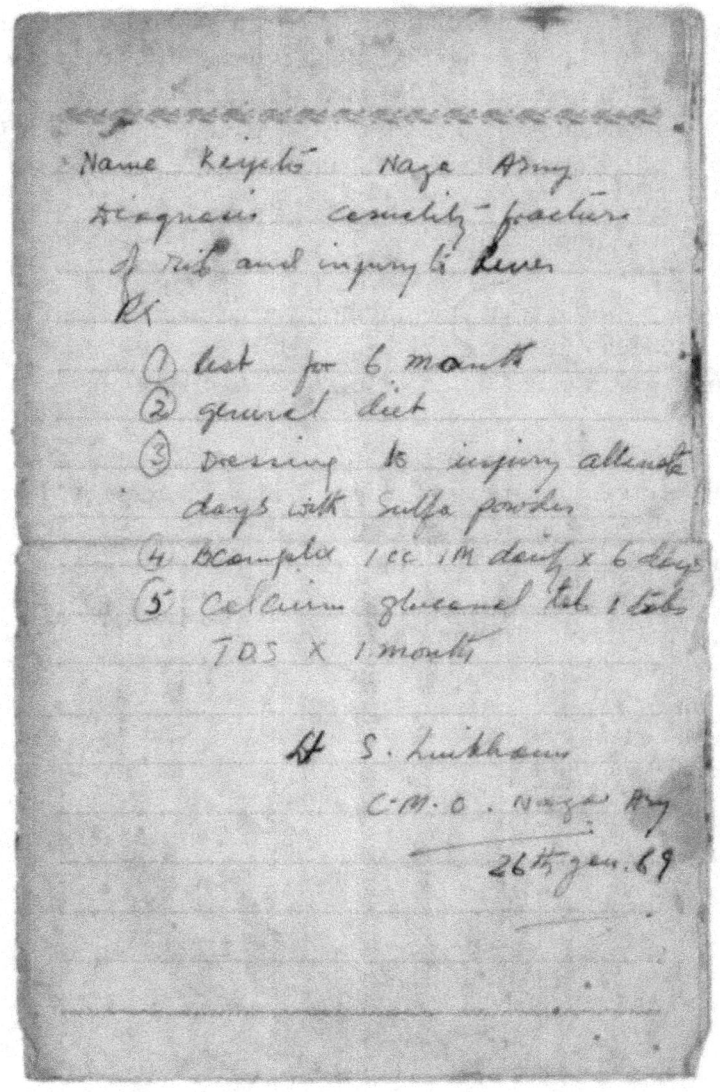

Lieutenant Dr. Luikham's prescription note for the injured Lance Corporal Kiyeto Sema

"Doctor, Sir, what's the status of the injured?" Raju Peyu Vihoshe Shohe requested for information. "With proper treatment and care, the Lance Corporal may fight back and come to live, but the Sergeant has only a short time before he soon closes his eyes," replied the doctor sadly. Raju Peyu Vihoshe was touched with emotion and anticipating that even the Lance Corporal may not survive, asked, "Boy, do you have any message that you would want me to convey to your family members back home?"

Raju Peyu Vihoshe cried when he heard what Lance Corporal Kiyeto Sema answered him in his sick bed. "Tell my parents and my love to pray and await my return, for I shall recover and be home again."

Lieutenant Colonel Lhouvicha Angami handed them 300 rupees each before bidding them goodbye. "Son, keep these 300 hundred rupees with you. Get well soon and we shall meet again. We shall be waiting for you at home," said Lieutenant Colonel Lhouvicha Angami as he handed the money to Kiyeto. Later, on 20th January 1969, Isak Chishi also sent him 100 rupees, along with a letter through a Kachin messenger, which he received on the 29th May 1969.

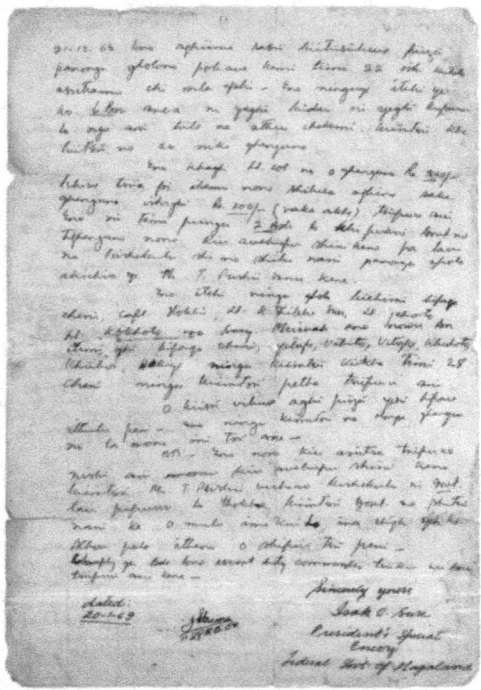

Isak Chishi Swu's letter to Lance Corporal Kiyeto Sema

Kiyeto Sema often dreamt of meeting his love again: the girl he had married just a few months prior to the mission.

"At a Kachin village in China borders, a KIA Captain's wedding reminded me of my wife back home, and it kept me braving all odds to be back home with my love again," wistfully recounted Lance Corporal Kiyeto Sema.

He was later taken back to China for medical treatment, recovered, and walked back home along with Th. Muivah, General Secretary, NNC.

Lance Corporal Kiyeto Sema of Sheipu village under Zunheboto district belonged to the 12th of 4th Brigade, 2nd Division, Central Command of Naga Army. In the mission he was assigned as bodyguard to Captain Yeshiho Awomi, the Command Adjutant.

Allow my love to end her wait

The column could no longer continue their stay at the village, for they had to move homeward towards the river Mali-hka. However, with enemy still attacking them fiercely, Sergeant Shikuto of 12th and Lance Corporal Heqhezu of 4th Brigade, decided to go into defence. "Heqhezu! Come, let's go and defend our men. The enemy has reached us again," Sergeant Shikuto called out.

"Is it unto death that we shall never forsake each other under any circumstances?" questioned Lance Corporal Heqhezu. "Yes, my friend," agreed the Sergeant, and the two began walking up the hill.

"Heqhezu, where are you heading without my permission?" shouted Captain Yeshiho to his bodyguard. "Captain, Sir, I shall be back soon," replied the Corporal.

"Make sure you come back soon and unhurt," said the Captain.

Sergeant Shikuto narrated the following to Sergeant Honivi as the latter attended to his wounds at a village. "At around 4:00 o'clock in the evening, as we lay in wait in defence on a slope, the enemy with a military hound swiftly crept down. Lance Corporal Heqhezu and I shot down the first two enemy soldiers along with the hound, but a bullet from another enemy soldier bore through the muzzle of Heqhezu's gun and killed him instantly."

Sergeant Honivi Yeptho, Clerk, 4th Brigade staff recounted the following: "In the morning, at the Command Adjutant's camp, Private Yamlu Tikhir was carrying water in a bamboo tube and walked past comrade Heqhezu, who woke up screaming. He had been sleeping beside Captain Yeshiho Awomi and me, and in a trembling voice complained that the Private had poured icy waters over his body. The unusual scream of fear he displayed in the incident had perhaps foreshadowed his death."

As Sergeant Shikuto, having avenged his friend, picked up the fallen and tried moving to another secure place, three lethal shots from behind riddled the right part of his chest and injured him gravely. Private Zuheto Chishi of 12th and another comrade shot down the enemy and under their covering fire, Corporal Vitoje retrieved the injured man. "Had it not been for the body of my buddy Heqhezu, I would never have been injured. I have fulfilled the vow I made to him, and I am happy for that," said Sergeant Shikuto on being rescued. Sadly, here again the body of Corporal Heqhezu could not be fetched back due to indiscriminate firing from the enemy side.

As Sergeant Honivi negotiated with the people at a Kachin village across the Mali-hka river for medication and treatment necessary for the two injured men, Sergeant Shikuto conveyed his last messages: "My friend, please tell my parents not to worry, for I have sacrificed my life for the Nagas as promised upon my entry into Naga Army; and please tell Brigadier Kivihe to kindly fulfil the words he assured me. May God protect and bless the command," softly uttered the Sergeant. "Please tell my love to end her wait for my return; tell her that I am sorry I could not keep my promise, that she should marry someone else and live happily," quavered Sergeant Shikuto, with tears coursing down his reddened cheek.

"Sergeant Shikuto also sent his Chinese pen, photos and his notebook to his fiancée; but what saddens me to this day is that, due to unpleasant circumstances I could neither convey the message nor deliver the things," lamented Sergeant Honivi.

Both Sergeant Shikuto and Lance Corporal Kiyeto were too injured to be carried along, so they left them at Umaka village on 23rd November 1968. However, the next day a messenger from the village conveyed the news of Shikuto's death.

Southern Command sends reinforcement

The Southern Command, on noticing the upsurge of battle at the village, sent a reinforcement of one platoon under the command of Captain Sanguto Chase of 4th and Captain Sakolie Yokha of 5th Battalions. They could not reach the village where the last section of the rear-guard was battling. However, the men displayed great courage as they engaged themselves in the fight which ensued until dusk. As they approached the fight scene, swarms of enemy bullets constrained Captain Sanguto Chase to order his men to withdraw back into the jungle. "Retreat and take cover in the jungle!" cried out Captain Sanguto and provided a covering fire for his men.

Captain Sanguto, a brave and selfless leader, chose to protect the lives of his men while risking his own; but before he could move himself to safety, enemy bullets forced him into a hollow ditch that could scarcely keep him from the bullet. With bullets whizzing above his head, he could not even move his hands to reload his gun, for any movement was a threat to his life.

He was left in such a situation that only God could save him. As he prayed to God in his time of unimaginable distress, he heard a voice distinctly calling his name there in the midst of firing sounds of bullets and 60 mm mortars. At first, he ignored the voice; but he was called out for the second time. By then he felt an inspiration so strong that bullets flying above him could not stop him from rising up and running for cover into the jungle. His men were awestruck when they saw their

Captain alive and unharmed. "Later that day I discovered that nobody from the unit had called out for me. I knew then that it was God who called me out and protected me from death," gratefully narrated Captain Sanguto Chase.

Private Sailanbo Liangmai explained how he had volunteered to join the reinforcement unit that day but was rejected. "Captain Sakolie Yokha refused, saying that I was too young to understand war tactics of foreign armed forces in a foreign terrain," said the Private. The Captain had not wanted to put the Private's life at risk. Private Sailanbo Liangmai, son of Gizanthuing Liangmai of Intuma village, belonged to 4th Battalion, 1st Brigade of Southern Command. He was just 14 years of age when he marched to China. The soldier boy of the mission was already 64 years old when the author interviewed him.

The Southern Command that had already crossed the river Mali-hka realised that the rear-guard, the Central Command, was taking heavy enemy fire, and sent another unit of reinforcements; unfortunately, they could not cross the river back to the battlefield.

The sky was full of choppers sent to rescue the fallen and wounded

In the battlefield beyond the Mali-hka river, around thirty Naga Army could not cross. As they fought the enemy till 6 o'clock in the evening, the growth of darkness ushered in the menace of crossing the rough and fathomless waters at night. In an attempt to restrain the Naga armies' further escape beyond the river ahead, and also to snipe at them, the Burmese troops even fired three to four Vereylights to light up the area. However, the boulders on the riverbank misled the eyes of the enemy soldiers. Hungry and intensely fatigued, they spent the night on the opposite bank of the river Mali-hka. "From the jungle, we saw the lit sky of dusk back in the battlefield," said one of the veterans, Corporal Khamkhui Tangkhul of 7th Battalion.

Next morning, the men moved upstream of the river, prepared bamboo rafts and crossed it. Alongside a few Kachin boatmen and fellow friends, 2nd Lieutenant Zhehoto, despite being tired, would not rest till all the troops were able to cross the river. That day, the command could see Burmese choppers busy ferrying their fallen.

The command, through its military assessment, could make out that the Burmese were intending to annihilate them between the two rivers, the N'Mai Hka and the Mali-hka, where retreat or cover was almost impossible.

However, due to their bravery and God's providence, the Burmese suffered huge casualties of more than 80 personnel (confirmed through KIA military intelligence and the second visit to KIA 2nd Brigade HQ by Isak Chishi Swu on 20th December 1968), while the Nagas suffered casualties of four deaths and one injury. The number of casualties Naga Army suffered was little compared to that of Burmese Forces deaths.

The following day, the Burmese choppers were still ferrying their fallen, and the Burmese forces ran amok after losing so many soldiers in the battle of Nchunglova yang. "When we attacked them with 60 mortar shells and automatic machine guns, we could hear screams and clamours of the Burmese soldiers. That day, they surely must have suffered colossal casualties with scores of deaths," narrated the veterans.

The battle, however, gave birth to suffering, hunger and considerable pain for the Nagas. It was the first fight they engaged on their way home, and thereafter the Burma land became a forest of foes and hunger.

The Burmese attack formation was so well engineered that it took at least three to four fights for the Nagas to make out their effective war plans. While they engaged themselves with the attacking party, another column of agile soldiers would be near them, attacking from the rear and mid-way. The Burmese soldiers were so well-trained that it caused a lot of problems for the Naga Army during the six months journey.

At Nchunglova Yang, the command was temporarily de-linked into as many as four groups-Isak and Mowu's group that had gone to KIA Camp, Colonel Lhouvicha with over 100 men as advance guard, men of Central Command that could not cross the river the previous night and

45 reinforcements from Southern Command as one group and around 46 others that were separated from the group and left unorganised.

Shall we go forward or backwards?

That battle at Nychunglova Yang triggered a fierce response from the Burmese authority and they gave their utmost in hunting down the Nagas by attacking them from both the rear and the front. The Burmese even engaged their military hounds. On 25th November, the enemy pursuit team attacked the rear-guard of Colonel Lhouvicha and his men on the bank of a rivulet. Sergeant Honivi, 4th Brigade Staff, Corporal Nihozu, 11th with Corporal Ghohuto of 12th and Private Khunito 14th all fought and resisted the enemy at the rear but became de-linked from the column.

They were left behind, stranded and reeling in the unknown jungle for five days; but the sunrise of the sixth day brought a surprise. An idea struck one of the men. "Sergeant Sir, we are now far from catching up with the column. We cannot go forward for we are massively outnumbered, and it is suicide to remain stranded here any further; for we shall soon run out of food and starve to death," cried Corporal Nihozu.

"I agree, Corporal Comrade, but what shall we do?" questioned Sergeant Honivi Yeptho.

"You have the guide map with you, so why don't you lead us back to China?" responded the Corporal excitedly.

The two other comrades also liked the idea, so they sat down and began working out the plan. Just then, a few Kachin people ran into them and took a quick and surprised retreat, mistaking the four Nagas for Burmese soldiers. The two Kachin words that Sergeant Honivi knew, saved them from missing their guide into KIA camp. As those Kachin people began fleeing from them, the Sergeant cried out at the top of his voice, 'Anthe Ni' meaning 'it is us' in Kachin language.

The men immediately stopped, turned back and said, "Many Buma (Burmese for Kachin people) soldiers have just gone the other way." These men then led the four Nagas into a KIA camp from where they could later re-join Isak Chishi Swu's column. (This was during Isak's second visit to the area.)

A ball of fire hit his head

During that separated period of time, Colonel Lhouvicha and his men, a little over 100, marched ahead without the rest of the column. In a jungle before Gumshen, a Kachin village, on the 27th day of November, 1968, Burmese Special Forces that had lain in waiting, ambushed and shot down three brave Naga soldiers; Sergeant Major Ketoulhoulie aka Azie, son of Menyio of Kohima village, Corporal Mezhüzolie, son of Kuolievi of Kohima village, and Private Zhaloupra, son of Lhoupulie of Kohima village. They belonged to the 6th Battalion of 2nd Brigade, 1st Division, Southern Command.

Later that day as the Colonel's men neared Ngakhet village, Burmese Forces opened fire and sent one of those balls of fire right into the forehead of 2nd Lieutenant A.R. Aso Tangkhul as he tiptoed before Corporal Khamkhui. The Lieutenant was not only a compounder of the command, but also the Company Sergeant Major of the 7th Battalion. He had saved many others' lives before he gave his own.

"I saw the Lieutenant fall right before me, and all I could do at that moment was fire back. I hurriedly picked up his gun and submitted to the authorities," said Corporal Khamkhui Tangkhul, son of Mayaothei of Ramvu, 7th Battalion, Southern Command, a veteran who walked just behind the Lieutenant that moment.

Blood - shed for liberty

On the other side, Central Command men and the reinforcement party of Southern Command would soon re-link with Isak and Mowu who were returning from KIA Camp. The combined team soon caught up with Colonel Lhouvicha's party and from there, they walked together again. Isak Chishi took a step forward and listened happily to his men's accounts of success in the battle of Nchunglova Yang. However, he lowered his head when they told him of the death of four heroes and one mortal injury. Isak bewailed the loss of his men and sadly uttered, "May the blood you shed bring liberty to the Nagas."

Supernatural help

Lance Corpral Ahoto Sumi aka Ishe, of 14th from Mishilimi, was also de-linked from the command. At a river he attempted to cling on to a slippery rock, but failed three times. He was so worried, for he did not know how to swim, and his only chance to survive the waters was to jump over the boulder which he had already failed to manage three times.

In his troubled time, he remembered his mother's words: "Son, when you are faced with a grave situation in life, always remember to say, "Praise the Lord", and God will take care of your problems." At the fourth attempt he succeeded when he jumped shouting, "Praise the Lord", but he lost track of his comrades and was left alone stranded in a deep jungle. The Corporal was exhausted; but as he rested upon a rock, in a trancelike state a man appeared and showed him the way he should follow.

Surely, it did lead him to his comrades the next morning. As Mrs Eustar Chishi Swu, President of CNC, NSCN/GPRN (IM) and the wife of Late Isak Chishi Swu, Chairman of NSCN/GPRN (IM) narrated the incident, Sergeant Tokim Tikhir remembered how he almost mistook and nearly shot the Lance Corporal for an enemy soldier when he approached the group that early November morning of 1968.

Rescue of four East Pakistanis

A week after this battle, the Nagas stumbled upon a small opportunity to pay back their gratitude to East Pakistan, (present-day Bangladesh) the nation from which they had taken aid before China. Four East Pakistan nationals were awaiting their arrival at one Kachin village, to march home under their care and protection.

Mr Bashid Ahmed, son of Mohamad Usan of village Chaphaudiya, East Pakistan, Mr Siddique, son of Bashir Ahmed of village Surburng, East Pakistan, Mr Munir Ahmed, son of Amin Sharief of village Surburng, East Pakistan and one other, all four of them were businessmen who had ventured into Burma, had been captured and imprisoned. After four years of imprisonment they were released from jail but never allowed to walk free; instead they were used as porters for Burmese Special Forces, to run errands for soldiers in their fight against the Kachin Independence Army.

In one such incident, the Burmese Forces came under heavy fire from KIA troops and were forced to take cover. In a chaotic moment, an escape route opened up, so leaving their baggage, the four Pakistanis fled the scene and escaped to a nearby Kachin village. "They were linked with us by the KIA and we took them and assured them of a safe return to their country when we reach Nagaland. They happily marched along with us unto the dark end," say the veterans.

CHAPTER 8
The Enemy Awaits

On the early morning of 3rd December 1968, the command reached Putao road, the road that connected Putao with Sumpranbum. It was an old horse trail used by Japanese porters during the Second World War that had come to be used by the Kachin people of the surrounding villages as a footpath.

The ambush

At the peep of the day, with faint visibility as they walked down the sloppy road, Burmese forces staged a surprise attack and forced the Naga Army to fall back. Some soldiers even left their baggage and ran for cover, despite the orders from General Mowu to stop running. Under heavy enemy fire, the command was left in a position where retaliation was almost impossible. "Do not run, do not run, I said do not run!" yelled General Mowu as he retreated with some of the baggage.

The attack could have gone too badly for the command, for they were within a whisker of being devastated; but three men from central command turned the tide by charging the enemy and helped blunt the attack.

The 2nd Lieutenant Yekhalu Jimo and Private Pukhashe, of 14th who had already taken position on each side of a huge tree, hit back. They were flanked by Sergeant Major Kivije Sangtam of 11th on the other side. While they provided a covering fire, others managed to take position and together they repelled the enemy from the ambush site. The trio's quick retaliations provided cover for the command men to regroup and engage the enemy.

Promised promotions

The General was aware of those who left the scene leaving their baggage, because he himself had collected some. He was very much aware of the situation that would have resulted, had the three not been able to retaliate against the enemy that morning. The bravery and quick response from the three earned the General's commendation. He was so pleased, that he noted the names and ranks of the three in his notepad and assured promotion and commendation once they reached home.

"General Mowu assured us of promotion and commendation, and we were very happy about that; but the government back home received us with bayonets instead of awarding citations for gallantry, and had us bartered off into the enemy's hand," lamented second Lieutenant Yekhalu Jimo.

"Chief Mowu assured me promotion on reaching home, but unfortunately I got separated from the General's group, as I followed the President's Envoy and never met the General again," sadly reported Sergeant Major Kivije Sangtam of 11th Battalion, Naga Army No. 4397.

Burmese Forces' second attack

After repelling the enemy forces, the command regrouped at a hill ramp a few hundred feet above the ambush site. There was a complete respite for almost three hours and the command was made to believe that the Burmese forces had withdrawn, so they had relaxed. Some were even having their morning meal when the Burmese who had regrouped themselves shocked them with another onslaught. In the second attack, the Burmese looked to overrun the Nagas with an improvised formation, with attacks directed from three directions making it difficult for the Nagas to manoeuvre the fight. Although it was not their terrain, the Nagas themselves being native to the hills and terrains like those of

Burma land could easily adapt to the condition. They fought back ferociously before moving off from the battle field in two groups.

His last morsel of rice

Private Khiungmong Tikhir of Anadangrü village was enlisted as one of the 4th Brigade staff in the command. He was a young yet daring soldier. On that day when they were attacked for the second time at the hill ramp, Private Khiungmong Tikhir was among those who were having a meal. He had eaten only a morsel of rice from his mess tin. He threw down the rice and, lifting his rifle, quickly engaged in the fight and ferociously hit back at the enemy. Private Khiungmong Tikhir displayed courage and agility before he fell to an enemy's bullet that killed him instantly. "The fight was so intense and the enemy's bullets so indiscriminate that we could not retrieve our fallen comrade's body," Sergeant Tokim Tikhir sorrowfully narrated.

Private Piwoto Sumi, Ighanumi of 14th Battalion, went astray from the command men while running for cover, and was captured along with the wireless set he had carried. He was then used by the enemy to track down the command men. The Private was later released into an Indian jail from Myanmar.

Another bullet finds its target

Private Yutsumong Tikhir of Chomi village, another 4th Brigade staffer, proved to the command leaders his worth, when he did not shy away from the chaos of the unprecedented attack carried out against them. The Private daringly threw himself into action, which luckily did not last long enough to cost his life, because not long after he swung into action, an enemy shot found its way through his bullet pouch and injured him.

With blood oozing from his body, the Private moaned, "Comrades, I am hit." He could no longer continue the fight, and was evacuated to safety by his comrades.

2-inch mortar lands in the midst of command leaders

Before the Burmese forces released their attack, the command leaders had gathered to discuss some important issues. 2nd Lieutenant Zhehoto Awomi described how a 2-inch mortar fell amidst their leaders that day. Isak Chishi Swu, the President's Special Envoy, General Mowu, C-in-C and the Command Commander, Colonel Lhouvicha Angami, the Command 2 I/C, Captain Yeshiho Awomi, Command Adjutant and a few other officers were all gathered when the incident happened. Had it burst, it could have left the command and the mission devastated even before they could reach home.

Command splits into two groups

The attack was so sudden and unexpected that it forced the formation of the command to split into two groups. Around fifty men led by Isak Chishi Swu moved back and went a separate way from the command.

They moved further into the jungle, took refuge there for a few days and went on to cross Putao Road on the 13th of December 1968; but were forced to make a tactical retreat, as the enemy lay in wait.

The team was further reduced to just 28 men when they were ambushed. Another group of 22 men led by 2nd Lieutenant Zhehoto Awomi and Honrie Muivah Tangkhul, the Personal Secretary to C-in-C, went astray from the team when they were attacked by Burmese forces.

Leaves over a fallen comrade

Isak Chishi Swu walked back to Brigadier Zau Tu's camp. During his stay there, all those that had gone astray were re-linked with his group. Together, along with KIA soldiers led by its leader Brigadier Zau Tu, they revisited Nychunglova Yang village, the first battlefield.

As they approached the village, Isak and his men were saddened to come across a noisome corpse of Corporal Heqhezu, whose body the Nagas could not give a proper burial. The awful-smelling remains prevented them from coming near, but Isak plucked some leaves and laid them over the body, prayed for his soul, and sadly moved forward.

His last resting place

When they reached the battle site, a few of the village menfolk guided them to the place where Corporal N-Nungrhomo Lotha had last fought. Isak and his men were told that the soldier was found dead in a shallow fire trench, so they had buried him at the place where he had fallen. "Burmese soldiers eagerly took turns holding the fallen soldier's gun before it was finally taken away by their leader," continued the men.

Surrounded from all sides

The other group of around 190 men, led by General Mowu, marched homeward fighting through and treading the northern route, luring the attention of the Burmese forces all the way to the borders of India and Nagaland.

Ever since the battle of Nychunglova Yang, the command had been hit with temporary separations and a few groups were yet to catch up with them, while a few others were left stranded either at Kachin villages or KIA camps with little chance of relinking with the command.

General Mowu had perhaps expected that Isak and his men, with the rest of the Naga Army, would soon be able to link up with his team; but that never happened. An inconvenient state of affairs prevented it from happening. Thus, from there on, the General and his 190 brave men fought all the way through the dense jungles, icy rivers, mountains and hostile terrain of Burma land with the enemy hot on their tail all the way home.

CHAPTER 9
Courage in the Face of Adversity

The Taron river ambush happened on the 21st December 1968. The river Taron, also known as Turong, is one of the tributaries of river Chindwin. It originates from Ngalang Taung and flows through some part of Kachin land before it confluences with the Chindwin.

Three days prior to the Taron river ambush, the Burmese had already collected enough information on the command's movement and her strength. They had cleverly tricked the Nagas into buying rice grain from one of their spies disguised as a civilian boatman. The Nagas, who were running short on food supplies, were unaware of the ploy. As a matter of fact, they did not even care much; they were just glad they could replenish their ration. They believed that the man was a civilian who had done business with them, for they trusted the KIA guides who made the arrangement.

Another goodbye

A few hundred metres before the Taron river, Private Woipu Sumi of 14th of Tsaphimi village, who had been seriously ill grew too weak. Constant hunger, lack of proper rest and the malevolent sights of the dense and rough forest deteriorated the Private's health. The command leaders, sensing that it might be too cumbersome for the men to carry the Private in the thick and unknown jungle terrain, suggested that the man be abandoned.

"The command wanted to leave Private Woipu somewhat earlier, but Lieutenant Yekhalu said that he would never leave any of his boys in the jungle to die. We continued carrying him for almost two weeks until that morning of 21st December 1968, when he could not even speak anymore. We knew he would soon meet his Creator and to continue carrying a tall and a heavily built man as he was, hindered our progress severely," narrated Private Lhoxuto Assumi of 14th Battalion.

"We laid him on a tarpaulin and left him with a faint hope that the party behind would find him. But the money and a handful of rice that we left beside him was just a desperate attempt to boost his morale or rather, a final goodbye. We knew beyond doubt that those materialistic things meant nothing to him anymore; he had even lost his senses by then. After about a furlong march, we were in for another surprise," narrated Private Kivito Achumi and Private Akhalu Assumi of 14th Battalion. Both men are from Natsumi village.

The surprise

It is a popular belief among the Naga warriors that instinct often speaks to the experienced and the brave. They use it to intercept dangers that lie ahead and thus prepare themselves to proceed cautiously. That morning, as they stepped upon the banks of river Taron, Lieutenant Yekhalu who was among the advance guard recalls how his face and ears would suddenly go warm, preceded by an eerie silence. He could sense that something unpleasant was about to happen to them. The sudden and unusual cries of crows in the area earlier that day had made him anticipate the presence of the enemy ahead, lying in wait for them.

General Mowu, the Commander, looked through his binocular over the other shore but the enemy defence that lay well camouflaged beneath the green leaves and grasses deceived his vision. He was confident that they were absolutely safe to wade through the waters; but the enemy bullets would soon prove him wrong.

Entering dangerous water

Men of 10th Battalion led by Captain Kochu Pocury stepped into the river as a vanguard followed by 11th and 14th Battalion men of Central Command.

Captain Kochu Pochury, a brave and upright man from Yesimi village, was a 4th Brigade staffer. In the mission he was assigned the Adjutant of Group A / Central Command. When around 25 men had entered the river, the Burmese forces opened fire and left the Naga Army men of Central Command in a dangerous position right there in the middle of the waters, with very little room for manoeuvre or retreat. Captain Kochu Pochury, who had already crossed the waters, swiftly took position on the riverbank and retaliated with his AK-56 and silenced the position that was attacking the men which provided enough time for the Captain's men to retreat.

However, the wrath of death still lingered around the men, for an enemy machine-gunner positioned just above the first attacker, released the second wave of fierce volley of shots whizzing above and near their heads. Without a covering fire, all those retreating would have been killed before setting their feet ashore.

"We must provide covering fire or all our comrades in the waters shall perish," cried Captain Sanguto Chase to 2nd Lieutenant Khrielakuo of 6th Battalion from Kohima village. The two fired from a position behind a big log lying on the riverbank. That gave the Central Command men enough cover for retreat.

Another soldier down

As the men in the water retreated under the covering fire provided by Southern Command comrades and Captain Kochu, who had by then already joined the men in retreating; Ghujukha Sumi of Mishilimi, a Private belonging to 14th was hit on the back side of the neck.

"I am hit," whimpered the Private, and his lifeless body splashed into the cold water of river Taron.

"As I bent over to pick up his arms, Captain Kochu ordered me to move forward. He brought the arms himself, risking his own life," narrated Private Akhalu.

Miraculous escape from the jaws of death

Every battle or war spares someone to tell a miraculous story. The fight had perhaps marked Corporal Zuheto Lukhami of 11th as one of the few that was blessed with miraculous survival in the incident. As they were retreating, an enemy bullet hit Corporal Zuheto's rucksack.

For a moment he might have thought he was done; but the enemy bullet had only hit the backpack, in which he had packed his loaded AK Magazines. When he searched his pack later that day, he found the bullet hit the magazine and saved his life.

Indiscriminate firing of light machine guns, combined with the shelling of 2-inch mortars by the enemy, caused the Naga soldiers at the bank of the river to suffer heavy casualties. Sergeant Renthungo Odyuo, of 17th Battalion, Central Command, recalled how the gravel in the shore had turned into bullets and shrapnel themselves when hit by the bullets and 2-inch mortars of the enemy.

The 2nd Lieutenant Yekhalu Jimo, while appreciating his Angami comrades, stated, "Had it not been for a vital covering from the Southern Command behind the river and also from the brave Captain Kochu at the river bank ahead, all of us in the water would have perished."

The Southern Command men who provided a safe passage for their comrades back into safety from the clutches of dangers in the waters could not, however, protect themselves from the wrath of death; they suffered at least four casualties.

A foreign land receives another Naga

Private Teisovilhou Angami of Kijümetouma,, from 6th Battalion, was bravely fighting alongside Captain Sanguto Chase and 2nd Lieutenant

Khrielakho, when he was hit and died instantly in front of Captain Sanguto, who saw him fall to death. "The Private could not even utter his last words or wishes," said Captain Sanguto. He gave his life in a foreign land with the hope that his people back home would live in peace and liberty. Brave comrades of the fallen, after a tough fight, retrieved the body and buried him there on the riverbank.

A Corporal succumbs to injury

Corporal Khiezeilie Rutsa aka Azei of 6th from Kohima village, suffered mortal injury when an enemy bullet hit his right buttock and entered the abdomen. Captain Sanguto under the covering fire provided by Captain Sakole Yokha and his men administered first aid and left him at a KIA camp. "The next day KIA messengers informed us that the Corporal succumbed to his injury the previous evening," Captain Sanguto sadly narrated.

Injured and wounded

Corporal Sobunuo, Lance Corporal Suolahie, Private Lhoxuto and a KIA soldier were injured and left at a Kachin village from where the VDF (Village Defence Forces), a local militia of Kachin Independence Army, escorted them to 6th Battalion HQ of KIA commanded by Brigadier Zau Tu, in Hukwuang valley at the borders of Naga areas in Kachin land.

A KIA soldier was hit on his heel and was carried away to their camp by Lieutenant Jacob and his comrades who returned from the river back to their camp. KIA guides left the Nagas after this battle.

Corporal Sobunuo Angami of 6th from Kohima village, suffered injury in the wrist and was left at a KIA Camp. On recovery later, the Corporal joined Th. Muivah's group and walked back safely to Nagaland.

Lance Corporal Suolahie Angami, of 6th Battalion, from Kohima village, sustained waist injury but recovered. The man also joined Major Vedayi and Captain Ihoshe for a second trip to China in the year 1972, but during their return journey he was killed in an ambush at the borders of Nagaland. "Lance Corporal Suolahie constantly expressed happiness at the fact of nearing home before we were ambushed in the borders of Nagaland," recounted Private Lhoxuto Assumi. The man was perhaps destined never to see his home again; but certainly, he had longed to see the freedom for his countrymen. Liberty for the Nagas is what he gave his life for.

Private Lhoxuto Assumi of Kichilimi village was only 20 years of age when he was commissioned for the mission. He was one of the youngest among the 14th Battalion. When he was injured on the left calf, Private Ivulho Lohe Lazami of 14th administered first aid. Along with Lance Corporal Suolahie, he walked to China for the second time and returned to Nagaland after receiving six months of training at Kadumkai in China.

To tread the trodden or the untrodden path?

Private Mhasilie Meru, son of Kru-u Meru of Khonoma village, was one of those who had volunteered to accompany Captain Lhouneizo of Rüsoma, (both of 6th) on a detachment to the ambush site. When the fight was over, the command pulled back into the jungle, but the General found that some of the men were missing. General Mowu detached Captain Lhouneizo Angami to bring back the men.

As the Captain and his men stealthily moved towards the ambush site, Private Mhasilie Meru stepped on a mine and was killed, with his right leg blown off. The Captain and his men buried the man there, and moved on with heavy hearts.

The fight at Taron lasted for over an hour and the Nagas fared very badly against the Burmese. Although the number of casualties was not exceptionally high compared to the first battle; yet in this incident there were not many confirmed kills from the enemy side as was in the first. The command here sustained eight casualties with four deaths.

The Naga Army could not break through enemy lines that day, so they moved upstream and spent the night in the jungle. That night, while most of the wearied soldiers were deep in slumber, the command leaders spent a sleepless night figuring out the best route for the command.

General Mowu had to take a quick and a sage decision. To take the normal route where villages and ration would be available would also mean to invite the danger of untold enemy attacks. To follow a new route would mean to bulldoze through the thick and rough jungle terrains, the dark and perilous forest of Burma land where neither rations nor a village was near.

General Mowu and his officers finally took the line of least resistance by taking the jungle route, laying stress on the safety of his men. Little did they comprehend the deadly condition the foreign forest had in store for them.

When they next opened their eyes, the soldiers failed to notice the immense pain and hunger that beset them. Canopies of the forest trees prevented them from beholding the darkened skies on the horizon.

CHAPTER 10
Hunger – The Enemy Within

The 22nd day of December 1968 led them into yet another formidable enemy to battle with; a battle which perhaps a number of soldiers were not prepared for. One cannot fight hunger with guns or artillery; it is but a battle that can be triumphed over only with patience, determination, self-discipline and a commanding will power. They suffered ten days of tears, hunger and painful starvation that Christmastide, in the hostile jungles of a foreign land.

The jungle, despite being a dense and virgin forest, could not provide enough food for the men. Even the edible wild leaves that were known to them became treasured trophies for the advance party and the rear-guard often had nothing to relish in those alien jungles. When the rest of the world was lavishly feasting on ambrosial Christmas dishes, the men had to fight starvation in the hostile jungles. Some had to settle with wild leaves, while a lucky few relished raw salty crab.

Few tried certain itchy leaves which are normally consumed back home, popularly known as "Kumthopiye" in Sumi dialect. They boiled it in their mess tins, but it was too itchy for consumption. That was one hungry Christmas they had.

Inconsiderate trio that sold monkey meat

On 26th December, the command men were surprised when a Corporal and two Privates belonging to 12th of Central Command began selling lumps of monkey meat (three pieces wrapped in a leaf) at 50 Rupees to their own starving comrades. The notorious trio had hunted down a monkey against the wishes and the order of General Mowu, their Commander. The Corporal even had his gun butt broken when he attempted to kill the monkey that was shot down injured. The General was extremely disappointed with their behaviours, because their gunshots aided the enemy in tracking them down at an easy pace and inflicted huge casualty to the command.

Having walked on empty stomachs for over a week now, some of them could no longer handle the extreme level of physical pain and hunger. A few of them stayed back, and met their end after the command men had walked a short distance.

Private Thüleytsü 10th of Phokhungri, was one of those who could no longer lift their feet even for a step. He had stayed back despite his comrades' call to move forward. "We persuaded him to push ahead when he showed signs of staying back, but he was too weak to walk any further. He sat down and was never seen again," said Lance Corporal Shutümi Jororr, 10th Battalion of New Phor village.

Private Ghujuhe Futhena of Lazakito, 14th Battalion, unable to bear the pain and hunger, gave up and fell to the ground to rest; but his commander, Lieutenant Yekhalu rebuked him and said, "Now, get up and follow me if you wish to see home again," "It is because of my commander that I reached home alive," gratefully explained Private Ghujuhe Futhena, who was attached to the Lieutenant as his personal attendant, before and during the entire mission.

Burmese Forces capture Five Naga Soldiers

The men were so overcome with extreme pain and hunger that one could have easily knocked them down with a feather. While the men continued to push themselves, one Yamukam Tikhir of Sangkhumti village, a Private belonging to 4th Brigade Staff, Central Command, could no longer continue to walk and fell to the ground. He was joined by four comrades, viz. Private Pfucha Angami of Kidima village and Private Vitsomo Kense of Tuophema village, both from the 6th Battalion, Southern Command, Private Avito Sumi of Ighanumi, 14th Battalion, Central Command and Private Athimbo Liangmai of Intuma, 4th Battalion, of Southern Command. They were soon captured by the Burmese Armed Forces and used as a means to track down the command men.

Climbing trees was our only option

Private Zuheto and his comrades could enjoy banana stalks which they came across on the 28th day of December. Meanwhile on the other side, the Southern Command had to bid a tearful adieu to one of their ailing comrades, Private Viyiezo, son of Lhoukienyü of Jotsoma village. The Private, who belonged to 4th Battalion, 2nd Brigade, was unable to move any further, so the General and his men bade him goodbye. One can hardly imagine the hopelessness the Private must have felt when enemy pursuit soon caught up and shot him to death (as reported by those who escaped later).

The jungle was dense enough to shield directions and coordination from the command men's naked eyes, so they often had to send men up the hefty trees to get a view. On one such incident on 30th December (the tenth day of hunger) in the afternoon, both the Central and Southern Command sent their men up the trees.

Soon a soldier from Southern Command shouted in excitement, "There's a paddy field up ahead!" The command therefore, set on the march towards that patch of jhum land up in the hill, with a great expectation that the field would have something in it for the men to eat. As they neared it they could see smoke coming out of the hut of that harvested jhum field. It sure did provide something in the likes of pumpkin, white gourd, tapioca and yam; but the rear-guard yet again stood no chance in finding any before the starving men of the advance guards.

Exhaustion on every side

As they rushed up, extreme hunger forced Sergeant Major Luvishe of

Surumi, 4th Brigade Staff, to lie down. The high level of pain caused his mind to play tricks, with the thought of surviving the ordeal.

"Sergeant Comrade, keep pressing forward, for it would be an impossible task to pull yourself up once your muscles are relaxed," advised Private Zuheto of 12th Battalion. However, the weak and exhausted body of the Sergeant Major was deaf to the Private's advice.

The Private had not gone far from the Sergeant-major when two enemy soldiers slipped down a crag and killed him. Private Zuheto shot down both the enemy soldiers and charged ahead. "Moments later, General Mowu walked up with the weapons of the enemy and the fallen comrade," said Private Zuheto Chishi, "and together we walked up the field," continued the Private.

Inquiry about the monkey meat

Up in the field, Private Zuheto was lucky enough to find a remnant of white gourd that lay hidden beneath the hay. He cut it into two and shared it with the General. "Chief Mowu at first refused, but I insisted," said the Private.

As they relished the gourd, General Mowu cleared his throat and asked, "Now tell me soldier, who was the man that broke his gun back in the forest? You must also give me the names of the other two that sold monkey meat." "General, Sir, I do not know the men, I have no clue of the incident," lied the Private.

Sergeant Tokim Tikhir also recounted how the General was generous enough to share the white gourd with him when he first reached the field. Sergeant Tokim and his men soon entered the hut and found nothing but a wild banana flower which they half roasted and ate along with water, just to fill their empty stomachs.

We stuck together

Private Tsoselie Seyie, son of Kenhiekhe Seyie of Tuophema village, a soldier from 6th Battalion, had also stayed back in the jungle before reaching the jhum field. "We waited for our comrade in the jhum field, with tapioca, but he never turned up," recounted Private Resietso Kense, of the same Battalion from Tuophema village. "Most men of Southern Command had a good practice of sticking together village-wise rather than in company, unlike the Central Command men during the times of attack," continued the Private.

Private Resietso Kense and three other veterans from the village, viz. Sergeant Major Khrutsolie Ziru, Private Visiekhrie Kense, and Private Rüzhükhrie Kense all from 6th continued the account; and said that a man who later joined the group reported that Private Tsoselie Seyie was found lying dead on the way.

11th Battalion suffers three casualties

Meanwhile, on the other side of the field, when the sun was setting, three Private soldiers of 11th hurriedly savoured a raw yam, then descended to a lowland in search of water; but they were attacked by the enemy. Two of them were shot down and the third injured. Private Tsoingki Samphury of Langturü village and Private Tsangkimung Samphury of Longkha village were killed instantly; Private Seksenthe Samphury of Longkha village sustained minor injury. The injured Private somehow escaped into the command and reported the loss of his fallen comrades and their arms.

At the village - New Tikhao

The advance guard had taken their meal by the time the rear-guard arrived at the village. The Commander-in-Chief, being aware that some of his boys were left behind, detached four men to the field with food packs. Private Zeneipra Angami, of Chiechama, 6th Battalion, Private Vihekhu Sumi of Sukimi, 4th Brigade staff, Private Yamlu Tikhir of Chikipongru, 4th Brigade staff and Private Vikiye Sumi of Iphonumi, 14th Battalion were sent, but were engaged by the enemy and could not reach their comrades. Private Zeneipra was killed in that gunfight; the three others reached the command unharmed.

At one of the messes, having detailed Private soldiers for cooking, Sergeant Tokim was unhurriedly changing his clothes. Duty commander of the day, Corporal Zuheto Lukhami of 11th on seeing the Sergeant half-naked, rebuked him for being too relaxed even in the middle of a battle. "Tokim, unless you have a plate of quartz on your forehead, you should not be as easy a target as you are at the moment," Corporal Zuheto rebuked his friend. "Hurry up, get dressed and take position before the enemy enters the village."

Tokim replied, a little wryly, "My friend, do not fear, for I am sure it is cattle that must have fooled you." "Private Tsungkimong!" called out the Sergeant, "Am I right?"

"Yes, Sir," responded the Private without much choice; and while still stirring the curry he was preparing, the enemy opened fire and injured his right palm.

"Is everything okay, Sir," queried Private Khiunga as he swiftly crawled in. "I am fine," shouted the Sergeant, but ordered him to take care of Private Tsungkimong's injury. Private Khiunga immediately tore the Private's shirt and bandaged the wound.

The Burmese forces, having captured five starving Naga Army who were found to be too weak to fight back, must have thought that the whole command was vulnerable to an attack and hence could either be captured or wiped out. The Nagas on the other hand, led by war-hardened commanders and senior officers, proved their readings wrong. Fate too had perhaps frowned on the Burmese that day, because when they charged the village at around 7 o'clock in the evening, they suffered heavy casualties. Many fell to the machine-gun shots and the thundering rage of mortar shells and RPGs.

The blow here was so heavy that the Burmese were sent wobbling back into retreat. They were sent into such a chaotic state that they even failed to manage the five Naga Army they had held captive, and gave room for two of them to escape: Private Avito Sumi of Ighanumi, 14th and Private Athimbo Liangmai of Intuma, 4th Southern Command.

Later that night, 30th December 1968, to wash their embarrassment off their defeated faces and to avenge their fallen comrades, the Burmese stooped to the level of dishonouring humanity. The highly disciplined Burmese forces unethically executed the remaining three Naga Army instead of holding them as POWs, viz. Private Yamukam Tikhir of Sangkhumti village, 4th Brigade Staff, Central Command, Private Pfucha Angami of Kidima village, and Private Vitsomo Kense of Tuophema village, both from the 6th of Southern command.

Although the enemy was repelled from the village, the command had little luxury to halt for the night there at the village itself. The commander and the officers knew how dangerous it would prove for the command to halt the night, as most of the men, having enjoyed a heavy meal after ten days of extreme starvation and lack of proper sleep, would soon fall into a deep sleep. The Nagas therefore, moved up to a hill beyond the village and rested for the night, before they lifted their feet for Old Tikhao village the next morning.

At Old Tikhao, Private Pukhalu Assumi aka Akhalu of 14th Battalion, who had sustained injury on his left ankle, could not walk any more. "Son, you are aware of how exhausted your comrades are and we both know that you on your own can walk no more," said Captain Yeshiho to Private Akhalu. "You must therefore take refuge here and come back home after you recover," continued the Captain.

A few days later, the villagers there escorted him to another Pangsha Naga village.

"Brothers, kindly escort me to a Sumi village near Ledo in Assam," requested Private Akhalu. "Okay," nodded the men; but they took him to Jairampur instead, informed the Assam Rifles there and betrayed him into the enemy's hands.

The ultimate enemy that defeated many Naga Army here was hunger; and of course, Mother Nature that added to their misfortune with alien jungles that had very little food for the men to survive.

CHAPTER 11
Death and Casualties Surrounded Us

On the 3rd day of January 1969, they moved out from Salung village and arrived at a small stream by late afternoon.

When the sun had begun to set, the men had prepared their meals and decided to settle down for the night there at the river bank. However, trouble soon set in when the enemy who had followed them caught up and attacked them. In the fight that lasted just about 15 minutes, the Nagas promptly hit back.

"Mortar squad, shell them out," ordered General Mowu. "Yes Sir," shouted the squad, and fired three shells. The mortar shells, combined with massive gunfire, inflicted heavy casualties upon the enemy. The KIA intelligence also reported that the Burmese commander of the day got killed in the bombing.

Nonetheless, the Nagas had to move out to another place.

Not long into their march that fateful night, the advance guard was ambushed by the enemy forces. It hit them like a thunderbolt because they knew of the enemy behind, but to be ambushed was totally unexpected. Private Visizol Ltu aka Tehibu of Kidima village, 5th Battalion, who was among the leading men, became the first victim of the ambush.

Captain Sakole Yokha of Kigwema, 5th Battalion, narrated how he, for a moment, was intimidated when Corporal Pfülhuvi of Sechüma, and

Private Letyo Angami of Rüzhaphema, 4th Battalion, were both taken down right before and behind him respectively. The Captain was so shaken with surprise that he burst-fired over two magazines of his AK 56 without even crouching.

"Sakole, ceasefire, retreat and take cover," shouted Colonel Lhouvicha Angami of Pfüchama, from behind him. "I am on the third mag, Sir," shouted back the Captain with intermittent lights still twinkling at the muzzle of his gun. "Everybody has retreated; I am the only one covering you. Now get back immediately and that's an order!" sternly ordered the Colonel.

"Okay, Sir" said the Captain and retreated. He modestly said, "I would have easily been killed that night had it not been for God's providence. It is neither my strength nor my goodness, but God's grace that I am still alive today."

The ambush had already cost the lives of three Naga Army in quick succession. Worse still, Captain Neilao of Kohima, 6th Battalion, another war veteran from Southern Command, sustained severe injury. The General and his men attended to his wounds, carried him for a while and left him at a village. He later arrived home safe with another group.

The next day when all the men had long gone ahead, the Central Command men manning the rear position planted a mine bomb at one strategic point where they had anticipated the enemy would follow. Before long, the bomb went off with a loud scream that sounded like that of the Nagas.

Captain Yeshiho immediately detached Sergeant Zhosal Angami of 5th Battalion, Private Zuheto and Private Zuhei of 12th Battalion, and said, "Go check the man and see if he is one of us."

On reaching the scene, they were horrified to see Corporal Yasie-o Rio of Tuophema village, 6th Battalion, whose both legs were blown off and had sustained injury on his hands too. Sergeant Zhosal and the two soldiers tried carrying him for a while but they knew that he would not survive; so they laid him between the roots of a big pipal tree. The Corporal sensing his end, made a rather unpleasant request: "Sergeant Zhosal, please shoot me," begged Corporal Yasei-o Rio in pain. "I can never do that; and you will be okay, so calm down my friend," replied the Sergeant sadly.

"I know I shall never survive and the pain is unbearable so please shoot me now," pleaded the Corporal again. Sergeant Zhosal, grieving, placed a shawl over his body and bade him a tearful goodbye.

Unknown to the command, Corporal Yasie-o Rio, who was de-linked from the command, had been trailing behind when the incident happened. He was a brave son of Kezocha Rio of Tuophema village, who, as a national worker, was serving as a Rana Peyu in NNC at the time his son had embarked on the Mission.

Sanching forest camp

Early morning of 7th January, 1969, General Mowu moved his men out from Sanching village and led them into a deep forest, where he had intended to establish a temporary camp. Once in the jungle, they came upon a place which was not the best, but a considerable one.

The place happened to be an old and deserted camp area of ENRC. The area was filled with edible leaves which are commonly consumed in Nagaland. The Sumis call it ghughuye: a type of itchy leaves used as vegetable in Nagaland. The Sumis of the command therefore nicknamed it as 'Ghughuye Camp'; and to this day this is how those veterans refer to the camp.

Captain Yeshiho Awomi, the command adjutant, announced: "General Mowu, our commander, intends to hold this area as his base camp to facilitate Chairman Mao's policies and tactics. He has therefore issued a stern warning against moving out of the camp, or venturing into the villages or jungle to hunt, without his due approval."

In about a week, General Mowu called a few of his officers and awarded promotion to around 60 Naga Army. Men of Southern Command like Sanguto Chase, Sakole Yokha, Megosazo and a few others were promoted to Captain from a Lieutenant, whereas the Central Command men were not immediately awarded.

A few officers of the Central Command inquired of Captain Yeshiho Awomi, the Command Adjutant who represented the Central Command and in whose care the promotion orders were given, as to why this might be.

The Captain, however, replied, "We have officers and soldiers who have received double promotion. We also have men who deserve a demotion and a few others who even deserve capital punishment. I shall therefore, reveal the promotion only at the reception at home." Unfortunately that never happened; hence Central Command men could not ascertain their promotion, with the exception of few who later got it confirmed from the General himself.

On another day, a Private from Central Command and two other soldiers from Southern Command ventured out to the village, and through them the enemy spies tracked down the camp. General Mowu grew boiling mad on learning of the trio's disobedience. He was furious at them for having disobeyed his orders. Given the circumstances, it was not impossible for General Mowu to pronounce capital punishment for the three; but the General's kind nature and forbearance under an extreme provocation allowed him to avoid the capital punishment which many believed they deserved. The General just caned them and pardoned all three.

On the 10th day of their stay at the camp, to the great disappointment of General Mowu, the Burmese forces launched attack. Corporal Tsangkhuchu Samphury, 4th Brigade staff, Private Mlayi Samphury of Langturü village, and Private Luashemung Samphury of Lamrorü village, 11th Battalion, who were manning the outpost, bravely fought back and shot down the first three enemy soldiers who approached the camp; and collected their arms.

In the attack, the Burmese suffered heavy casualties: as many as five deaths and more injuries; but the Nagas could not hold their camp, so they abandoned camp and moved towards home once again. The Nagas in this particular fight did not suffer any casualty at the hands of the enemy.

However, the command in this forest area had to meet disappointment after disappointment. Disappointment for the southern command for suffering the huge casualty of five deaths and one injury; disappointment for the Central Command for failing to ascertain promotion which they well deserved and had so wanted to know; and, most importantly, disappointment for the General and his officers by the act of a few irresponsible soldiers that foiled their plans.

CHAPTER 12

Please Don't Leave Me Behind

Before the joint ambush at a Konyak village, they were attacked by the Burmese at another Naga village. In the attack, three Naga Army were killed, viz. Private Lhousakhonyü of Jotsoma, 4th Battalion, Private Esol Angami of Khuzama and Private Kenihosa Angami of Kidima, both from the 5th Battalion. Colonel Lhouvicha Angami suffered minor injury, got de-linked from the command, and could catch up only the next day.

Though not heavily against the Nagas, several villages were slanted towards the Burmese forces. Perhaps in an attempt to please the oppressor and escape the wrath of her forces over their villages, the Nagas of Burma, time and time again, caused harm to their own brothers and sons by helping the enemy forces. An incident at Konyak village on 20th February, 1969, when villagers joined with Burmese forces to ambush the Nagas, is one typical of such cases.

As they moved up the village approach road, having crossed a rivulet, the three Khiamniungan civilian porters began yelling their war cry as though to give out signals, and escaped into the jungle, leaving all the baggage they had carried. Just then the enemy opened fire and injured two of the Naga Army.

The Nagas immediately retaliated and shelled the enemy position. Captain Sanguto, Captain Sakole and their men leading the advance guard shot down the three enemy soldiers that were leading the attack.

However, Sergeant Major Vitsolie aka Bvüu of Jotsoma village, 4th battallion, took a hit and fell down below the road, injured.

"I am still alive, please do not leave me behind," cried out the injured Sergeant Major. "Go get the man," Captain Sanguto ordered his men, and bravely charged forward.

On the other side, an enemy soldier bravely confronted the 14th men but he was soon outflanked and left injured. The petrified enemy soldier lowered his head into the makeshift bunker like a pangolin rolling its head for cover.

"Attack, brave men! Stab the enemy! Any man who does not use his bayonet on the enemy today shall miss recommendation in the record book," bellowed the Battalion commander, 2nd Lieutenant Yekhalu. "Charge!" shouted the men and released their frustrations and anger.

When everybody rebuked him for being too religious to stab an enemy, 2 I/c of the Battalion 2nd Lieutenant Yetovi Sumi of Ustomi, reluctantly stabbed the enemy soldier and created a moment that later would give the men some memories of laughter. He was an earnestly religious man and did not want to stab his bayonet on a helpless enemy combatant.

"Charge…. eisheili…. so, are you the one causing us troubles all along?" roared the Lieutenant and stabbed the enemy soldier just once.

Being heavily shelled and outnumbered, the enemy soon fell before the infuriated Nagas. They were overrun and, with the exception of those that escaped, all that came on the way of the Nagas were either bayoneted or shot to death.

Khrutsolie Ziru of Tuophema village, a Sergeant Major from 6th Battalion, still recounts the moments he bayoneted the enemy soldiers that particular day. "I have had enough of wars and there is nothing of it that enthrals me anymore. The one thing that but fascinates me is the moment we bayoneted enemy combatants at a battle in a Konyak village," remembered Sergeant Major Khrutsolie Ziru.

The Burmese even left the food they had prepared for themselves, a mixture of millet and job tears with tin fish that would provide a platoon.

Having vanquished the enemy, the Nagas regrouped and found that none had taken care of the fallen comrades that had cried for help. General Mowu immediately detached second Lieutenant Yekhalu Jimo and another officer from Southern Command along with 15 Naga Army to fetch the fallen. "By the time we reached the ambush site, Sergeant Major Vitsolie was killed with his hands and head cut off, along with the four other enemy combatants, by those villagers that had accompanied the enemy in the ambush," recalled Yekhalu Jimo.

Private Pusimo Kense of 6th Battalion, who managed to hide himself in a bush above the road, was retrieved by the men. He had suffered multiple wounds; both arms and both thighs were grievously hit, and he had suffered a lethal bullet in his backbone. General Mowu knew that the man would not survive, so he decided to keep him in the village at the Ahng's (Konyak Chief) house.

"General, Sir, how is my brother's condition?" anxiously asked the Private's cousin, Rüzhükhrie Kense of Tuophema, another Private of 6th Battalion. "He has received injury on his arms and thighs but need not worry for he shall recover soon," the General lied.

"I did not know that my brother had his backbone injured when I carried him piggyback to the Ahng's house. I trusted my General, and therefore, believed that my brother would soon recover," mournfully recounted Private Rüzhükhrie Kense.

"My brother, Chief Mowu says you will soon recover but you would need rest. We are therefore leaving you at the Ahng's house here in the village. Get well and we shall soon meet again," consoled the Private.

"It is okay, brother, but I am a little fearful of the threat these villagers pose," stammered Private Pusimo Kense. General Mowu, realizing the Private's fear of being killed by the villagers, spoke to the Ahng and conveyed a stern warning. "Should anything untoward happen to the Private, the entire village shall go down before the fire of the Naga Army," he cautioned.

Private Rüzhükhrie Kense bade a sad farewell to his cousin, hoping to meet him again.

Private Theingairio Tangkhul of Saikhor, a 7th man of Southern Command, also fell too ill to walk, so they left him at the village, "Friends, I have a feeling that I might get killed if I am left in the village; but I shall stay here, recover and come back to see you all," lamented Private Theingairio. "Amen, we shall soon meet again," replied Sergeant Samatai Luikham of 7th and his comrades. The Private recovered and returned to Nagaland in 1969, later joined NSCN IM but was killed in action.

On the 24th of February 1969, when they arrived at another Naga village, they were greeted by a man claiming to have just returned from China trip. "I am Lieutenant Niangba Konyak and I have just returned from China along with Brigadier Thinoselie," the man confidently introduced himself. "Boy, do not lie for the consequences shall be harsh," interrupted Captain Yeshiho Awomi.

"No, Sir, I speak the truth, Sir," resolutely replied the man. "In that case, sing before us any Chinese revolutionary song," ordered the Captain.

"Daxai xaishing kao doushou... *"Sailing the Seas Depends on the Helmsman"* sang the man, proving his claim. The command leaders then asked him to guide the Nagas home. Lieutenant Niangba Konyak belongs to Wukha village whose father was a Konyak Ahng of not only the village but also the region. He thereafter became one of the command men; he then led the command to another village called Lao.

CHAPTER 13
Do Not Shoot! I Surrender!

Before reaching Lao village on 26th of February 1969, a messenger from the village reported the presence of enemy soldiers.

Lao is a mispronounced version of the name Lonyu by the other Nagas. According to the Leinong Nagas, it is pronounced and spelled as Lonyu Noukgong. The village is mostly inhabited by Leinong Nagas with around twenty-five percent of the people belonging to Konyak Nagas. It lies in the Jekong range of Leinong Nagas under Lahe Township in Myanmar.

On a hilltop above the village, the Nagas planned an attack on the enemy and strategically descended in a three-pronged attack formation towards them. However, before they could reach the spot, the enemy had already withdrawn beyond the village and had hidden in a bamboo grove.

The enemy here was actually looking to avoid the Nagas, as the previous many ambushes and battles had shown them a clear picture of the Nagas' bravery, and how heavily armed they were. They had also made out that the Nagas had equipment much superior to and more sophisticated than theirs. Also, the number of casualties that they had suffered at the hands of the Nagas infused pain and fear in the hearts of this army, so that they had actually humbled themselves to safe havens when the Nagas came looking for them that day at Lao village. The Nagas, on the contrary, were by then filled with the highest degree of anger born of extreme pain and hunger and also of the constant attack by the enemy for the last four months.

The fight at Lao would not have happened if not for the Nagas who went searching for the enemy that had retreated. "Men, let's pull back. The enemy must have taken to their heels," shouted Captain Kochu Pochury. Just when they were beginning to withdraw, Lieutenant Nyukhapa Pochury of Melury, the unit commander of the 10th Battalion, spotted a group of enemy hiding in a mud cave a few yards below the bamboo groves.

The Lieutenant bent over and while pointing at the enemy said, "Look, there they are." Just then an enemy shot passed through the Lieutenant's neck killing him right away, and also delivered a severe blow to the Central Command by injuring the group's Adjutant, Captain Kochu Pochury. The Captain sustained injury on the thigh and buttock. "Get back and take cover, Sir" cried the men, and tried evacuating him.

However, the Captain, sensing the importance of a senior leader amongst his men to boost their courage and morale, refused immediate medical attention and continued guiding and cheering his men to charge forward.

"Brave men, leave me, I am all right," insisted the Captain. "Just charge in, I am right behind," he continued.

The Naga Army immediately fired back, lobbed hand grenades and silenced their guns. The effect was furthered by the RPG shot that was launched into the enemy hideout by Piwoto Sumi of Ghokimi, a Private from 14th Battalion. "Piwoto, quick, shoot the RPG!" cried out Sergeant Tokim Tikhir to the RPG shooter who was trailing just behind. "The men have taken down Lieutenant Nyukhapa and have also injured our Adjutant."

At the end of the shelling, Corporal Tokiye Sumi of Achikuchumi, 12th Battalion, and Private Vighozu Sumi of Sukimi, 4th Brigade Staff, charged in and bayoneted one enemy soldier that was found hiding beneath his fallen comrades' bodies. Had his gun not jammed, the enemy soldier would have killed them both. "These two bullets here meant for us have been deactivated by God's grace alone, my friend!"

exclaimed Corporal Tokiye Wotsa to his friend Private Vighozu, as he picked up the enemy's G-III rifle and checked it.

"Moments later a Burmese Army soldier who had hidden himself in a bush, surrendered to us," recounted Corporal Tokiye Wotsa, who was force-drafted into Naga Army by Captain Kiyelu and Lieutenant Avito at Yehemi village on 12th January, 1963.

The soldier who surrendered before the Nagas that day laid his gun upon his rucksack on the ground, unbuckled his belt, lifted both his hands over his head, and walked out of the bush from where he had taken shelter. "Hilamaat - do not move," bravely shouted Private Vihokhe Chishi as the man surrendered before the Naga Army. Private Vihokhe Chishi was a 15-year-old new recruit, and was just 14 when Lieutenant Hukiye of Kiyekhu village and Lieutenant Zhehoto Awomi of Lukhami, conscripted him into Naga Army on the 3rd of February, 1967.

Corporal Kichotsing Sangtam of village Natsami, 11th Battalion, rushed in. "When I snatched his bullet pouch, it had four magazines full of 9 mm shots, and the man had also carried a little rice grain wrapped in a piece of cloth; also some opium powder," he said. Sergeant Jehoto Tsuruhumi of 12th swiftly picked up the stengun that the man had humbly laid upon his rucksack on the ground before surrendering.

Private Kivito Achumi of Natsumi, 14th also narrated how he and Sergeant Jehoto Sumi Tsurhumi of 12th charged in along with other comrades before the soldier surrendered. Sergeant Tokim Tikhir also recalled, "When Piwoto launched RPG and the Nagas charged in, the man having no way for escape, surrendered by himself before the Nagas." "Central Command men have made us proud," exclaimed the Commander, General Mowu Gwizantsu, when they handed over the surrendered soldier.

Meanwhile, Private Thinuoselhou Angami of Rüsoma village, 6th mysteriously fell dead with no injury visible to his comrades, not even a drop of blood on his body. The fallen displayed neither entry nor exit point of any kind of bullet. "Check the man and ascertain the cause of his death," ordered Captain Sanguto to his men. The men quickly scanned the Private's body and reported, "We do not find any injury mark on the comrade's body, Sir."

"If there is no injury, the man must have died of a heart attack," Captain Sanguto kept mumbling to himself as he closely examined the Private's body. However, he soon discovered a tiny hole pierced through the Private's uniform just on the left side of the chest. The Captain and his men unbuttoned the man's uniform and found that an exceptionally small piece of shrapnel from a grenade had made its way into the Private's heart.

Meanwhile, on the other side, Captain Sakole Yokha was leading 2nd Lieutenant Yetovi of Ustomi, (14th Battalion), Private Sato Angami of Jakhama, and Private Nothul Angami of Chakhabama, (both of the 5th Battalion), when enemy bullet hit and injured his right shoulder.

"Why are you boys firing from behind," cried the Captain to the men behind. "Why would we fire at you, Sir? It is an enemy bullet that has hit you," replied the men and evacuated the Captain to safety. "Take proper cover and protect yourselves," cautioned the Captain as he was being carried away.

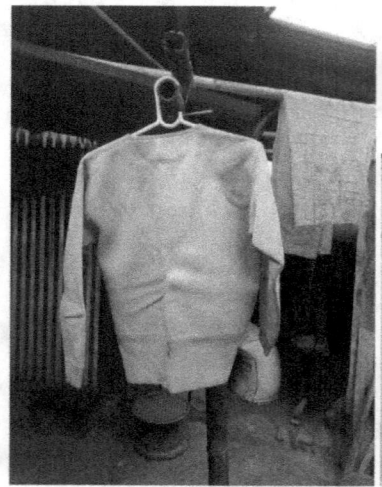

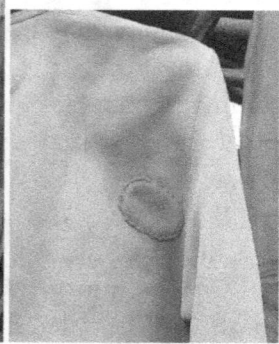

51 years after the incident the Captain still has his bullet-riddled uniform sweater which he has preserved as a souvenir

He later received medical aid from Colonel Lhouvicha Angami and Captain Sanguto Chase and continued marching with the command.

Sakole Yokha of Kigwema village was a brave Captain in the 5th Battalion, 2nd Brigade of Southern Command, Naga Army. He joined the Naga Safe Guard at Mima Camp on 27th February, 1956.

The Captain, who was born on 22nd February, 1937, enrolled into the Naga Safe Guard, in the month of February, 1956, and was injured on 26th February, 1969. He considers the month of February as very significant and co-incidentally related with his life.

When the sounds of the guns had died off and the enemy had long gone, the command regrouped and as they discussed, Captain Kochu Pochury expressed his desire to continue marching with the command despite being injured.

"Captain, you may not be able to continue the walk; so do you wish to be left at any village soon?" General Mowu asked Captain Kochu. "I am ready to die with the command but never will I stay back in a foreign land," firmly replied the Captain.

The Captain decided to continue marching alongside the command, but his injury left him incapable of performing the duties assigned to him as the Adjutant of Group A (Central Command). Captain Yeshiho Awomi, by order of General Mowu, therefore relieved Captain Kochu of his assignment. "Men, as you are aware, Captain Kochu's injury has rendered him incapable of performing his assigned duty as the Adjutant of Group A - Central Command. Therefore, the Captain is hereby relieved of his duty with immediate effect," announced the Captain. "By order of the commander, General Mowu, I hereby authorize 2nd Lieutenant Yekhalu Jimo, CSM of the Group A, to take additional charge of Adjutant till further order," he continued.

The Burmese Forces in the fight suffered yet another appalling blow; one surrender, seven confirmed deaths and scores of injuries, while the Naga Army sustained just three casualties, one death and two injuries.

CHAPTER 14
Almost Home

Tsonkhao was a delicate village built along the gentle slopes of a hill that stood parallel to another undulating hill on the east. The village, having a picturesque landscape, must have for a moment mesmerised the eyes of the Nagas when they first viewed it from the hill next to the village, but their minds knew of the grim brutality that the beautiful hill had contained. The Nagas were in fact prepared to attack the Burmese Forces' outpost that stood a few hundred metres above that village.

The attack was very crucial and indispensable to the command, because they had no other option than to bludgeon their way out through the outpost. Intelligence reports and the sources from the villagers proved to the command that they had no way home except through the village. They had to take the post at any cost.

To avoid any further bloodshed and also to stay away from disturbing the peaceful state of the village, General Mowu wrote a letter to the enemy outpost suggesting a cease-fire and to allow safe passage for the Naga Army that was returning from China. The Burmese, however, shied away from returning any response but rather showed signs of acute stubbornness and readiness to fight the Nagas. The outpost commander even tried to fool the General to send in men into his outpost to discuss. General Mowu had even deputed his 2 I/c Colonel Lhouvicha; but before the officer could move in, the Burmese Forces launched the attack.

The enemy in the afternoon of 28th February 1969, sent a wintry response with 2-inch mortars that hit the machang in the village where a few officers and soldiers were sitting. "Incoming, everybody take cover!" cried out a soldier, seeing a mortar falling towards them. The mortar drilled through the bamboo floor of the machang and blew off to a loud roar beneath the machang.

"Lord, I am injured and profusely bleeding; to give life and to take it is yours alone. Please, God, do not let this injury kill me here in a foreign land. Allow me to reach my home alive and I shall serve Thee; so please save me, Oh God," Sergeant Rengthuno prayed as he first-aided himself. Rengthuno Odyuo, of Yikhum village, a Sergeant from 17th Battalion, sustained shrapnel injuries on his left shoulder, left side of the buttock and on his nose. He still has a piece of that shrapnel in his left shoulder.

Private Rüzhukhrie Kense had a lucky day when the utensils he had carried prevented the impact from injuring him. "With all the utensils rippled, it is a pure miracle that I survived the attack without even a trivial injury," delightfully recounted the Private.

The Nagas formed a three-pronged formation and approached the outpost from three directions, with two groups directed at the north and south of the outpost and one at the middle in the east. The HQ party with General Mowu and some other command leaders were stationed at the village.

Private Khiungakiu Tikir aka Khiunga of Sangkhumti, 4th Brigade staff, who was among three other comrades who were tasked to guard the captive soldier, refused to listen to his company commander, Tokim Tikhir, and left his three other comrades viz. Private Iqheto Sumi of Sukimi, Private Yamlu Tikhir of Chikipongru and Private Chimthong Tikhir of Chikipongru, all from the 4th Brigade, to join those who were moving up to attack the outpost.

"Khiunga, why have you abandoned your friends? Go back and mind your duty," Sergeant Tokim reprimanded. "I joined the mission not to guard a surrendered captive but to fight the enemy, Sir," bravely replied Private Khiunga, and continued to follow the Sergeant and his men. "You must go back," repeated the Sergeant.

However, the Private, as if to say; a man destined to fall seldom reads the writing on the wall, was too stubborn to heed the Sergeant's order. "You always ask me to follow you wherever you go, why then not today?" insisted the Private, and forcefully joined the men.

As Private Chimthong Tikhir of Chikipongru, Private Zupongtsu Pochury of Sütso, 10th Battalion, Private Khiunga and Sergeant Tokim charged up the enemy outpost, Private Zupongtsu quickly positioned and with his LMG, silenced the enemy that was attacking them, but continued firing even after the man's bunker had gone silent. "Zupongtsu! Ceasefire, the enemy has already been silenced, now relocate immediately! The enemy must have marked your position," Sergeant Tokim cried out. The Private promptly crawled off but Private Khiunga in a flash jumped into the Private's position and got hit.

"Khiunga, what's wrong with you today? You look a little clumsy and not your usual self," Sergeant Tokim rebuked on seeing the private fumbling. "I am injured," indistinctly groaned the private and fell tumbling down the slope for over ten feet.

At another position, 2nd Lieutenant Yetovi, 2nd Lieutenant Yekhalu, Brigadier Prem Tangkhul and three of his bodyguards shared the same defence. Brigadier Prem, using one of the guns the Nagas had captured from the Burmese Forces, kept cursing the enemy. "Khamya bei twa malay? Where are you going?" the Brigadier abused the enemy. "Keisah meshi bu labah- there's no harm, come here," the Brigadier continued shouting.

"Brigadier Sir, please keep your head down. There's an enemy soldier sniping at us from a bunker below the one we are confronting," suggested 2nd Lieutenant Yekhalu.

The enemy combatant had positioned himself below a trench near a helipad; a few metres to the west of the position to which Brigadier was shouting at. "Yes, Sir, you must calm down and keep your head low," added 2nd Lieutenant Yetovi Sumi. Paying no heed to the advice of the two much junior officers, Brigadier Prem continued swearing at the enemy.

Finally, as he stood up cursing in Burmese again, an enemy bullet silenced his swearing for good. "I heard the bullet snapping into his left eyebrow, and right there between 2nd Lieutenant Yetovi and me, the Brigadier fell dead to the ground," recounted 2nd Lieutenant Yekhalu Jimo.

The three bodyguards, a Sergeant and two Privates, carried away the officer. Brigadier Prem Tangkhul was a brave officer in the ENRC organization. He had joined the Naga command to guide them home. He belonged to Somrah village in the Naga area of Myanmar.

Not long into the waiting, the enemy combatant's head bobbed up from behind the trench. 2nd Lieutenant Yekhalu took the man down and avenged the Brigadier. "Lieutenant, go get the man's gun. I shall cover you," exclaimed 2nd Lieutenant Yetovi, and provided covering fire as Lieutenant Yekhalu rushed up to the enemy's bunker. Lieutenant Yekhalu regretfully narrated how he had, not out of callousness, taken off the fallen enemy's uniform to give it to his clerk. "For a moment I thought I wasn't doing what a soldier is supposed to. The thought of laying at least a leaf over a fallen enemy combatant kept on ringing in my head, but the want of clothes by one of my men, Private Vikiye Sumi of Iphonumi, got the better of my scruples, and there was no stopping me from taking the man's shirt and trousers," plaintively explained the Lieutenant.

"May I keep the boots, Sir," requested a Private from southern command. "No, you may not," said the Lieutenant; but his acts betrayed his conscience.

Meanwhile, at the northern end of the outpost, some of the Nagas out of anger even thought of killing innocent civilians - an officer's wife and her daughter, who were left abandoned at the camp. "Let us destroy them too," shouted some soldiers, on seeing the two. "We will never allow you to commit such an act on innocent civilians," replied Private Zuheto Chishi. "Come, let us protect this woman and her daughter from any harm," he called out to his two other comrades. "Ok," responded Private Qhuhoi of 12th and Corporal Kushokha of 14th and together they held the house.

Corporal Kushokha and Private Zuheto did their best in gesturing the petrified woman and her daughter towards a seat. "Fear not, we shall neither kill nor harm you. Take a seat and relax," gestured the men. Private Zuheto quickly picked up the officer's helmet and wore it. As the three ate the officer's rice, Corporal Kushokha threw in a humorous punch line. "Zuheto, with that helmet on, you look like the officers who has just run for his life, leaving his wife and children into the care of enemy soldiers," Corporal Kushokha gabbled with his mouth full of rice. Just then an enemy bullet pierced through the bamboo wall and reached Corporal Kushokha; but the stock of his AK 56 prevented it from injuring his abdomen.

Later that day, when Private Zuheto descended with the enemy helmet still on, his comrades mistaking him for an enemy, almost shot him. "If not for the Chinese gun and the uniform, I would have become the target of my own comrade" recounted the Private.

"I must get a boot today or I shall suffer. The boots of the first man I kill shall be mine," Private Resiesto Kense of 6th from Tuophema village, murmured as he charged up the enemy outpost. Soon enough, the Private got his price, but removing tightly-laced boots cost him time, so he cut off the legs with his machete and carried away the boots along with the enemy's feet.

Back home and then, it was a normal practice for the Naga Army to take away the fallen's uniform and boots due to lack of inadequate supplies; therefore, it was not unusual for the Nagas to have done such acts even during the mission, especially when one ran out of clothes and shoes.

Corporal Karutsu Pochury of Sütso, unit clerk of 10th Battalion, was ferociously fighting the enemy when shots hit his bandolier and destroyed at least five of his bullets. He did not suffer any injury and bravely fought the battle till the end.

The attack was actually launched to create a passage for the command to head home; but as they gained ground, Nagas sought after other goals, like gathering enough loot for themselves by completely overrunning them. After a fierce and bloody battle, the Burmese post was eventually overrun.

The better equipped Naga Army, who were heavily motivated to fight their way home, was too strong for the Burmese Forces there to withstand, so they abandoned their post. It was a new but well-established post. It had freshly dug trenches running around the camp; it was also a chopper-holding post. The Burmese were hell bent to stop the Nagas from entering Nagaland in order to please its partner India; so they had built a new outpost to oppose the advance of Nagas into Nagaland.

The Nagas soon collected necessary food items and incinerated the entire camp, except for the post commander's house where the wife and a daughter were found hiding, terribly scared. Here, some of them snatched arms, helmets and even gold; but many were more focused on taking food items such as rice, dal, sugar, milk powder, etc. A Sergeant who found condensed milk carried it to Nagaland; a Private who found gold kept it until it was confiscated later.

In a little over 20 battles or gunfights with the Naga Army, the Burmese forces were outsmarted in all the fights and were left absolutely discredited with huge casualties, and the loss they suffered at the hands of the Naga Army of the mission from China.

The enemy receives a gift

General Mowu, though young by age, always demonstrated maturity in his decisions and actions. In the six days that the enemy soldier was held captive, none was allowed to mistreat the man. He was considered a POW and accorded all possible treatment of a military prisoner.

The General realised that it was a futile attempt to continue holding the captive: it made little sense, for they had then neared the borders of their homeland. Therefore, on the 7th of March, 1969, the man was unconditionally released from the clutches of Naga Army at a village called Mukhoji. "Please take me along. I do not wish to go back for they will have me executed when you send me back," pleaded the captive Sergeant. Colonel Lhouvicha cheered up the worried captive: "Fear not! Chief of the Naga Army, General Mowu has not only released you but has also kindly arranged two local men to guide you safely into your nearest outpost. Take these and go home safe," continued the Colonel, as he handed the man a sum of five hundred rupees and the General's hand-scribbled letter addressed to the Burmese Forces officials.

"You shot and injured me at Lao and here I am offering you my jacket; go tell your people of the love and kindness of the Nagas," said Captain Kochu Pochury as he smilingly handed the man his jacket.

The Nagas, unlike the brutal Burmese Forces who mercilessly shot down three Naga Army POWs at New Tikhao, displayed complete restraint in any form of physical or mental torture. Rather, the Naga Army treated the man quite well before releasing him.

The fight is almost done and soon our pain shall disappear into the skies, for beyond those blue hills, our brothers to honour us await our arrival. Soon we shall see our homeland and our loved ones. We are almost home.

CHAPTER 15
The March of Betrayal

Navigating the jungles of Penkim for the whole day, General Mowu and his loyal troop finally reached Pungro on the 12th of March, 1969. The General had intended to wade past Tizu river and thence safely into Chakesang region via Laluri, a Pochury village. A Lieutenant leading the advance group, on seeing men at the river through his binoculars, immediately reported this to the General; but he was ordered to march forward, with the reply that they could be civilians and there was no need to be too cautious.

However, when they had come fairly close to the river, General Mowu from behind saw the enemy and ordered immediate retreat. They took a detour towards Xutoi village, where they spent the night in the jungles of Shiphimi.

The Naga Army moved down the hill and up again, under full observation by the Indian Army at the river. Surprisingly enough, the command was just allowed to walk in and out freely without being confronted. Moving out from the sight of the Indian Army, the Naga Army forded the icy-cold waters of Zungki river, so that many of them reached Samphury village soaked and cold on that 13th of March, 1969.

Little did the enemy presence bother the Naga Army then. They were rather satisfied and convinced that they were just at the door to their home, expecting a jubilant and heroic reception. They were yearning all the while for the great day in their reception camp.

On 13th March 1969, at Honito village, Captain Pikiye Yeptho came looking for General Mowu and had a brief discussion with him. "Could you guide the command into Chakhesang region via Thakiye-Khiza?" General Mowu asked the Captain.

"Akijeu ("Sir"), all routes to Chakhesang area are heavily guarded by the Indian Army. The only safe passage that I could guide you through is into the 2nd Battalion Headquarters of Atukulo camp commanded by Colonel Zukiye Zhimomi," replied the Captain. "Besides, I have been sent by the Government to guide you safely into the camp," continued Captain Pikiye, and led the General and his men towards Yethumi village.

The Fight with the Assam Rifles

At Yethumi village, while the command men were busy cooking their meal, Assam Rifles from Seyochung post approached and opened fire at around 7:30 to 8:00 hrs in the morning. Soldiers of 14th manning the outguard post retaliated with heavy machine-gun fire, and also heavily grenaded the enemy forces. The Assam Rifles here suffered heavy casualties with at least two confirmed deaths and many injuries, and also lost an LMG and a rifle into the hands of the Naga Army.

Taking effective firing from all sides and being grenaded heavily, the remaining combatants were forced to take to their heels. The month of March being dry, the jungle soon caught fire and added to the advantage of the Naga Army. The Assam Rifles had not only to withstand the hail of bullets from the guns of Naga Army, but also the literal fire of the jungle that added to their quick withdrawal.

The Nagas knew nothing of this when they fought against the Assam Rifles at Yethumi. Having reached Nagaland, they had perhaps anticipated more battles with the Indian Army; but they never knew that they were fighting their last ever gun battle for their motherland. Greed of some leaders had perhaps prepared a dungeon for them to be contended with.

After the enemy had withdrawn, the Nagas moved into Tsunaki river below Kiphrie town, had their meal there at the river, and moved up to Kisetung village. When they arrived, Mr Tsutoho Sangtam and Mr. Tsapise, cautioned General Mowu from entering Atukulo post. "Do not enter 2nd Battalion of Atukulo camp. Those men have formed a Revolutionary Government and are no longer a part of the Federal Government of Nagaland. They have all become agents of India," Tsutoho Sangtam cautioned General Mowu.

"Where will you then keep these many armed men? In your villages?" thundered Captain Pikiye, sounding a little disturbed.

General Mowu and his men were as yet unaware of the development and the RGN's plan. They only knew that they were entering Colonel Zukiye's camp, where their faithful and brave General K. Zuheto Swu was awaiting their arrival from a foreign trip.

General Mowu, realising that they had come too far from re-routing to either Chakesang area or to any other safer place known to them, inquired of the two leaders, "Can you guide us to any safe place in these jungles of yours? I need a place for my men to take shelter before we move out into safety." "We do not advise this, Sir. The jungles here are unsafe; the Indian Army has cordoned off the entire region," replied the two.

Captain Pikiye was perhaps kept in the dark of the RGN leaders' plan when he was tasked to guide the General and his men into the 2nd Battalion Headquarters of RGN at Atukulo. The Captain narrated how he had to hastily rush down from a tailor's shop at Kiphrie town, leaving his half-stitched clothes, when he was informed of the arrival of the Naga Army from the Mission.

Captain Pikiye Yepthomi, son of Hevuxu Yepthomi of Sutimi village, who was enrolled into the Naga Safeguard on October 10, 1955, with No. 78 as his Army number, was a brave warrior who guided the Nagas of the Mission into the trap of betrayal. Although it is widely believed by many that the Captain was perhaps unaware of the treachery, yet he is considered unfortunate, for history has entangled his name to the wicked branches of the great betrayal tree.

Meanwhile, Captain Yeshiho Awomi, the Command Adjutant who had already met Colonel Zukiye in the camp, sent a message to the General that they were all clear to enter the 2nd Battalion Headquarters of Revolutionary Government of Nagaland, commanded by Colonel Zukiye Zhimomi. Leaders at Atukulo received the General and his men with kisses and hugs reminiscent of Judas and Jesus Christ; they were allowed entry only after forcing the General to sign a certain agreement, it is alleged.

That blissful moment of reaching home, however, was soon proven a disappearing joy; happy moments often come with wings; it always makes a hasty flight.

It is said that Colonel Zukiye Zhimomi allowed General Mowu and his men's entry into the camp, only after the latter signed that he had become a part of the Revolutionary Government. If it is true, the General must have done it to save his men and perhaps he had trusted the leaders in the camp. What ecstatic agony the General must have felt when he reached home, but had to plead for entry!

The General was told of the RGN only at Kisetung village, a day before they reached the 2nd Battalion Headquarters, but he had a firm belief that General Zuheto Swu would honour him and his men. Besides, there at the doors of the RGN's trap, his retreat was next to impossible. He knew well that would cost the lives of his men, so being left in a mire and with only a faint hope of rescuing his men, General Mowu hammered the last nail into the coffin by leading the Naga Army into the RGN's 2nd Battalion Headquarters, on 14th March, 1969.

On the first night in the camp, the RGN soldiers suggested that the Mission men rest from performing any sentry duty; but the brave men, despite being heavily fatigued, insisted and had a joint duty with the RGN soldiers. The next day, the Mission men were ordered to submit their arms and ammunition in the quarter guards for verifications and records. Being unmindful of their heinous plans, the Naga Army of the Mission faithfully submitted their entire arms and ammunitions; but what happened next surprised them all. All the arms and ammunitions were taken away by certain officials of the RGN, and the men were left empty handed.

On 16th March, 1969, when the sun in its fallen blaze had begun to descend into the horizon, darkness with its bosom companions, tribulation and agony, swooped over the brave men of the Mission. With General Mowu and Colonel Lhouvicha asleep in Colonel Zukiye's inner room, the tragic drama unfolded.

Handing over a hundred-rupee note to his clerk who had just entered his room, Colonel Zukiye Zhimomi ordered, "Lhojevi, read this into my ears, it's a note from General Zuheto." "Timi hipaqo phekivilo (do not set free these men)," read out the clerk. "You are being loud, just whisper it," cautioned the Colonel.

"The rest of the few words whispered into the Colonel's ears I could not hear, but I heard the first sentence," recounted Zuheto Chishi, a Private who was in the Colonel's anteroom the night they arrested the two leaders. A few moments later, three RGN Captains, a Sangtam, a Yimchunger and a Sumi, barged into the Colonel's inner room.

"Wake up, Sirs, and put your hands up; we have orders to arrest you, Sirs," the three Captains at gunpoint ordered. "What is going on officers, why arrest us?" questioned the General. "Akijeu ayehza ke- The law, we've been ordered, Sir," replied the men and duly arrested the two leaders.

The Federal Government of Nagaland may have failed to receive her C-in-C, General Mowu; but the General was happy that he had safely made it to the RGN camp with his men, undetected by the enemy. His tide of joy soon turned into waves of sorrow and pain.

The next day, General Mowu and Colonel Lhouvicha were flown down to Kohima, but the rest of the General's men were lied to by saying that they were being taken for a peace meeting at Chedema Peace Camp.

After a few days, the rest of the Mission men too were interned by the RGN soldiers; their yesterday's comrades-in-arms.

Finally, on the 20th March, 1969, the Naga Army of the Mission was handed over to the Indian Army. With over half their strength drained, they still forded the threatening waters of N'Mai Hka, Malikha, Tarun and Chindwin rivers, navigated the meads and stygian jungles of Burma, and braving many battles and unknown hostile terrains of an enemy-filled foreign land, these heroes marched home victoriously and were therefore expecting a hero's welcome. Alas! These Naga heroes in shining armour were betrayed and sent to be mere caged birds in the hands of the enemy by their own people.

Never did the RGN leaders want General Mowu and his men to perish. They valued their lives, but they helped the enemy to book them under the section of a code that awards death. Oh, what joy those leaders must have felt when they saved the lives of the General and his men! The men were neither betrayed nor bartered; oh, how pure and selfless leaders were they! But for peace in the Naga country, these brave soldiers of the FGN had to be betrayed into the hands of the enemy.

The men were ferried by chopper to Chakabama Army Camp on the 20th of March 1969, and their belongings were confiscated on 28th March 1969. The next day they were carried off to Diphu, thence to Hazaribagh[2] Central Jail, Bihar. General Mowu and Colonel Lhouvicha had already been taken away for imprisonment at Tihar jail.

---

2 Hazaribagh at present has become part of Jharkhand, a new state formed from Bihar

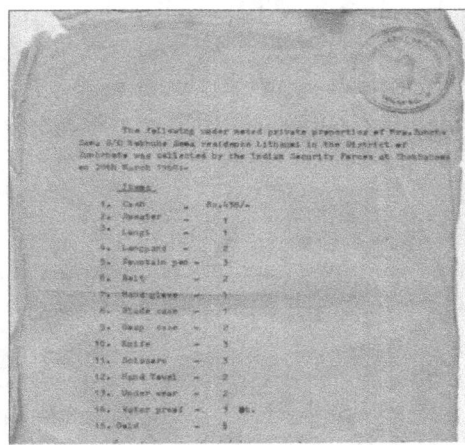

No we must not kill him

By the time Isak and his group reached Nagaland, Army jungle operations had been intensified with an intention to capture the rest of the Nagas that were marching along with Isak Chishi Swu. He finally had to part ways from his men at a barren jhum field below Shamator town in Tuensang district. Moments before they were captured by the Indian Armed Forces, Corporal Khamkhui Tangkhul, Sergeant Honivi Yeptho and a few others, tried somehow to persuade Isak Chishi Swu to escape. "Do not tarry any longer, Sir," strongly urged the men. "You must leave or get arrested, and that we cannot afford."

Finally, Isak, with two soldiers, sadly moved away.

"God certainly was with Isak Chishi, because the moment he began moving out with his men, a canopy of clouds clustered around them until they escaped into the cover of the jungle," recounted Corporal Khamkhui. Lance Corporal Khenchumong Tikhir of 4th Brigade staff, with another soldier; led Asu Isak towards his village, Shamator, and hid him in a barn where he ate, defecated and slept in the barn itself for three days.

Isak's stay there was, however shortened, when Mr. Khriero, the then Extra Assistant Commissioner of Shamator, declared a reward of rupees

200000/ (Two lakh) and a double barrelled 12 Bore Gun to whoever captured or aided in the capture of Isak Chishi Swu. Mr. Tsingthong, younger brother of Lance Corporal Khenchumong, immediately tipped off the announcement to Isak and helped him escape to Phisami village that night.

Mrs. Eustar Chishi Swu, wife of Late Isak Chishi Swu and the President of CNC, NSCN IM told how Isak had tried discussing with the RGN leaders in vain.

Having dodged through the enemy, Isak Chishi finally walked into the RGN camp, met with the leaders there, and reasoned that they had committed a blunder in having broken away from the national stream and the actions they had committed. Some of the RGN leaders however were annoyed and sought a way to kill him too; but General Zuheto swiftly intervened and discussed the matter with Colonel Zukiye Zhimomi, who said, "Pa pithi mulae apitinomu sake- We must keep him alive as seed saving."General Zuheto Swu therefore arranged two RGN soldiers to help Isak Swu escape from the RGN Camp.

Earlier General Zuheto Swu, in an attempt to prevent Mr. Isak from entering the camp, sent out Sergeant Tokim Tikhir to find him and help him escape. The Sergeant was handed a new five rupees note on which was written, 'Peace Mission Member', to be used as a pass to avoid capture by the Indian Armed forces. "Son, you are a hero; now go find Asu Isak and tell him never to enter Atukulo Camp," said General Zuheto Swu to Sergeant Tokim Tikhir.

Sergeant Tokim, along with Colonel Henito Kapo of Henito village, Captain Satovi of Shothumi, Limti Tikhir of Shamator, Khientsu Tikhir of Thonoknyu village and few others, boarded a chopper at Lukhami; but on landing at Thonoknyu, the Sergeant was captured by the Indian Army, who had been informed of his involvement with the Mission. His pass could not help him escape the Army.

CHAPTER 16
Your Reward Awaits

When they walked to the Middle Kingdom to free our land from a foreign grip, heaven knows they were unmindful of the liberty that they would never see, and even as they fought back pining for home, leaders in Nagaland may have connived with the foe and had a new home prepared for them. Therefore, on reaching home they were hustled into the dark corners of their new home; a house of constrained liberty sealed with iron bars, bereft of love and life of a world outside.

Hazaribagh Central Jail Bihar (1969-1971)

By April 4, 1969, at least 254 Naga Army men were left reeling in the solitary cells and wards of Hazaribagh Central Jail, Bihar (Jharkhand at present), isolated from their loved ones and the rest of the world. Their charge sheet soon arrived, and in the investigation that threatened their lives, many bowed before the enemy. Those men began proving their innocence; "We have undertaken the Mission at the General's and the government's behest, and we know nothing." Perhaps they could not remember that the Nagas were fighting the Indians for suppressing the Naga liberty.

However, one hundred and nine true and brave Naga heroes stood firm even before the face of death itself. "Why did you go to China?" questioned the investigator. "To procure arms and such other aids," bravely answered the Nagas.

"Why procure arms?" "To fight the enemy out, from our country Nagaland."

"Why procure arms?" "To remove the enemy out from our country."

"Who is your enemy and why?" "India, for suppressing our sovereignty."

"Why did you visit a foreign nation without the approval of the President of India?"

"We ventured out to a foreign nation under the supreme authority of the president of the nation we belong to, and not India. The question of permission from India and its president for us Nagas to visit any foreign nation therefore does not arise," replied the Nagas, fearlessly.

Surprise release

By December 26, 1969, in just eight months, Captain Yeshiho Awomi, the Command Adjutant and 144 others, were surprisingly released. The rest were detained under numerous acts, labelled as dangerous.

Perhaps it was too tough for India to retain Captain Yeshiho Awomi and 144 others because the Captain, unlike many other junior officers and Privates, was a mere Adjutant of the command, the man who was fourth in position during the entire Mission. The Captain and his men persistently told the truth in every investigation: that they had known nothing of the Mission but had just obeyed orders.

None pleaded or made a deal with the Government of India; but it was made impossible for India to not release the men. It was impossible for India to punish those who were ignorant of the law. The great Indian court had perhaps done away with the maxim *ignorantia juris non excusat*, for that purpose.

"Comrades dear, see you soon! It should not take long before you too are released," the men consoled those imprisoned for life. "Oh yes, it must not be too long we suppose. We just must spend one short period of life imprisonment with death not far behind."

"All right, take care. Any messages back home?" "Tell our people and loved ones to weep for us no more, for we too shall be home soon. We may not live to celebrate the sovereign Naga nation and its liberty, but we surely shall inherit the Sovereign Nation of Eternity."

The state of Nagaland appealed to the court that the arrest of General Mowu and his men had created a lot of commotion in the underground set up in Nagaland. It was therefore feared that if, for the purpose of and during the investigation of the case and for the trial, they had to be taken to the state of Nagaland, their presence itself would overcharge a situation. This would incite public movement and bring the administration into an embarrassing position, affecting seriously the operations of law and order.

The State Government was too scared to hold its own in its land, fearing that it might create an unwanted situation; and prayed the court to hold them outside Nagaland. The court, therefore, ordered that the case be sent to the District Magistrate, Nowgong.

According to the veterans, Hokishe Sema, then Chief Minister of Nagaland state, even stated that they were Chinese Communist-trained and therefore, like earthen pots, misshapen in a way that cannot be corrected, but has to be destroyed.

Nowgong Special Jail, Assam (1971-1973)

On 31st January, 1970, they were shifted to Nowgong Special Jail in Assam. For nearly two years the Nagas did not see their two leaders, but by the time they reached this jail they got to meet their two leaders, General Mowu and Colonel Lhouvicha, who were also transferred from Tihar jail.

By then there were 134 of them: 111 Naga Army of the China Mission; three of the four East Pakistanis who had marched alongside the Nagas from Kachin land in Burma; one made a lucky escape along with Private Kirisa Angami of 5th Battalion to his village, Kidima. Twenty of them were those Naga Army who were captured by Burmese Forces when they attempted to cross into China led by General Dusoi Chakesang. They were transferred from Agra jail to Nowgong Special Jail.

Why did they betray me?

General Mowu evidently had bitter feelings against his Sumi brothers for having him and his men betrayed into the enemy's hand to perish. One time, being overpowered by his emotions General Mowu unhappily expressed, "Semas are my enemy." 2nd Lieutenant Mesevi of Nerhuma village, 6th Battalion, quickly intervened, "Sir, in saying so you are being unjust to these Sumis who are here to perish alongside you." "I agree Lieutenant. I have just fallen before my emotions," said the General. In fact, he did really love and cared for the Sumis Naga Army who were with him.

"The General was exceedingly kind to us Sumis, especially when it came to the question of those that fought with him till the last moment in jail," declared 2nd Lieutenant Yekhalu Jimo. "General Mowu must have said that in frustration and emotion because some of his Sumi comrades back home betrayed him, and not that he was unhappy with us. In fact, he would always care and had special concern for us," said Sergeant Honivi Yeptho.

Soon, the charge sheet against them was submitted under Sections 120B/ 121, which is punishable with death or imprisonment for life. This is found in 121A/122/149 of the Indian Penal Code, under sections 7 and 8 of the Nagaland Security Regulation V of 1952, under section 13 of the Unlawful Activities (Prevention) Act, 1967, under sections 25, 26, 27 of the Arms Act of 1959, under Section 12 of the Passport Act, 1967.

"Friends, we have been charge-sheeted under sections of Indian Penal Code that awards death or imprisonment with life; but we must be brave, we must be resolute," encouraged the few educated Nagas of the 7th Battalion. "We have pledged to sacrifice our lives at the altar of Naga liberty. We do not fear to die for it," resolutely shouted back the Nagas

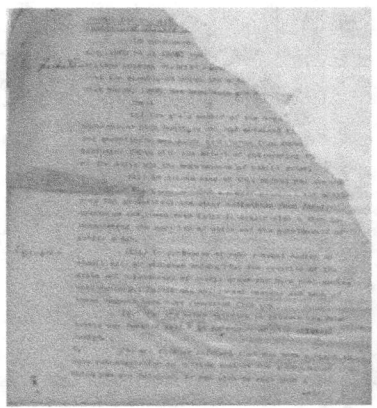
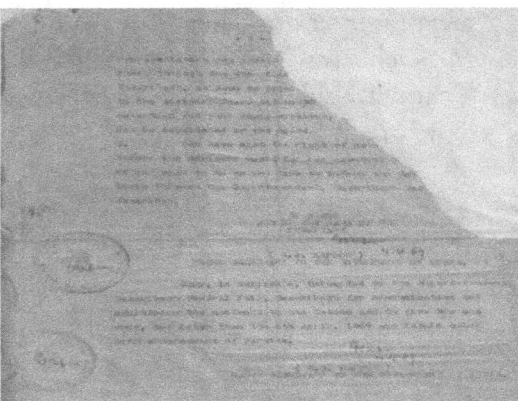

Page 1   Page 2

When notice of the rule was served on General Mowu and his men, the following helped the General in refusing to sign it, and instead wrote the following remark on the notice itself: Honrei Muivah Tangkhul, Lieutenant NG Phungshuk Tangkhul and LM Sanyi Mao, Publicity Secretary, all BA graduates while Lieutenant Doctor Samson Luikham Tangkhul a BHMS (Bachelor of Homeopathic Medicines) and a BSc in General Nursing.

State of Nagaland - versus - General Mowu Gwizantsu and 134 others

The remark read: "We have nothing to do with state government. We are struggling to regain our sovereignty suppressed by the Indian government. We therefore do not like to sign it."

Some days later, Nagas were denied rations and some other essentials for a few days. When they demanded it on 20th February, 1971, instead of meeting their grievances, the Assam police, led by the Superintendent Mr. Debisuvas Nedy and the jailer of Special Jail Nowgong, Mr Badan Chandra Phukon, bludgeoned them with clubs inside their wards and looted their belongings.

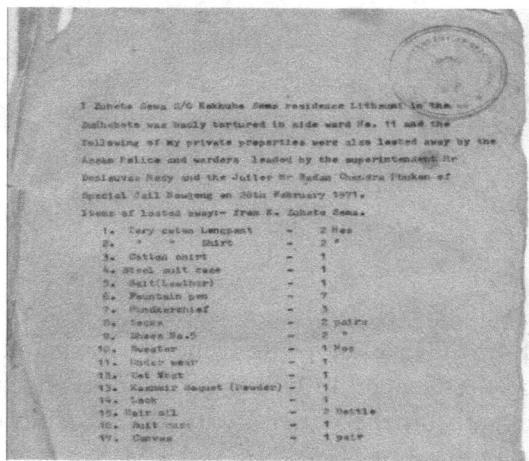

Not a soul was spared from the beating; 14 of them were hospitalized at Civil Hospital Nowgong. Corporal Tsawoto Sumi of 12th and Captain Ngutsonyu Chakesang suffered brain injury, while Sergeant Honivi Yeptho, who regained his senses at the hospital bed, suffered a head injury requiring three stitches.

A lover's letter

One summer afternoon, a jail staff member seated in the courtyard of the wards announced the arrival of inmates' letters.

"Boys, come out of your dens and shake your legs over here, you've got messages from home. Everybody! come and get your letters," he shouted, as he read out the names. In a wink, those whose names were read out swarmed towards the man's table. Each excitedly collected his own piece of love that had come from home.

Yekhalu, who had happily collected his letter, walked back to his ward a little worried, for he knew he could not read it by himself. He did not even know who the sender was; but deep in his heart he was quietly hoping that the letter was from his lover.

In the room Captain Tsupichu Pochury cheered him up and offered to read out the letter for him. He unfolded the letter, glanced over the sender's name and said, "Hey, Lieutenant, don't you wanna know the sender?" "Of course, I do, but I implore you to first read the letter and as you read on I am sure I shall come to know even before you finish reading the first line," smiled the Lieutenant.

The Captain smiled back at him, cleared his throat and began reading it:

June 3, 1971.

Dearest Ilomi,

I sincerely hope and pray that this letter reaches you in good health, as I am, in Christ. I should like to also tell you that I shall be sitting for the second terminal exams by the end of this month and all I want is prayers and good luck wishes from you my dear.

Although you did not mention anything of your Mission to China when we last met, you said you would be back soon for our marriage and I waited but you did not come. Oh, how could you have come when they had you arrested and imprisoned! Oh, dearest Ilomi, I really hope you are keeping well.

I do not know when fate shall smile upon our union but there is one thing I do know and I must tell you that I shall be waiting still, for you when you get back home. Till then take care until we shall be together again.

Your loving,
Alomi

"Take it, my friend," said the Captain with a smile as he handed over the letter to the Lieutenant. "Thank you very much Sir." Yekhalu took the letter, kissed his lover's name on it, folded it quietly, then kissed the letter and with a smile on his face, tucked it away beneath his pillow.

He spent the rest of the day in utter excitement. That night as he went to sleep, he dreamt of his fiancée bathing at the village well as he arrives home, cleansing off a baby's dirt from her back. "Oh, my dear, what are you doing here, and whose baby is this?"

"Oh, my dear, who could this be? It's our child! I am so glad you're home. I've been waiting for all these years."

"I am just home, and we are not yet married. How then could you have a baby with me? Honey, this is absolutely impossible."

The fiancée remains silent for a while and says, "Not a day passed that I did not think of you, and here you are to be with me forever. Oh dear, trust me, this is our child."

"You have cheated on me. How could you do this to me?" The Lieutenant woke up screaming and so disheartened.

Prison school

One bright, sunny July day of 1971, seated in a room with Sergeant Honivi Yeptho and Lance Corporal Thongtsi Tikhir, Yekhalu requested his friend, Sergeant Honivi, a sixth-grade graduate, to teach him how to read and write.

"My friend, days and nights come and pass, all things shall come and go as has been designed by nature; but, sadly, we may have come here never again to leave. I doubt if we shall ever walk out alive; but if there's ever a chance to walk out alive, I wish to meet my fiancée as a literate. I want to learn to read and write; I must learn. Will you, my friend, be kind enough to teach me?" Yekhalu earnestly pleaded with his friend Honivi.

"So long as we shall stay here together, my friend, I shall teach you with whatever little I know and you shall surely learn to read and write, God willing," replied Sergeant Honivi. "However, we have a little yet a big problem." "What is it?" "We do not have any of the materials required for teaching and learning, no pencil, no pen nor paper."

"I have an idea," said Yekhalu, as he rushed out of the room; and soon hurried back with a piece of colourful paper he had kept hidden underneath his mattress.

"What is this?" asked Honivi. "Condensed milk wrapper my friend." We can use the inner-side of it; it is blank. We can use it, can't we?"

"You have surprised me with your cleverness and a strong will to learn. May God bless you, my friend. However, we must get many more of those wrappers, and shall soon begin the class," said the Lieutenant's soon to be and first ever teacher, Sergeant Honivi Yeptho.

"Excellent, Sirs, I shall also join the class, please accept me too!" exclaimed Lance Corporal Thongtsi Tikhir.

"All right then; shall we go get more wrappers and borrow a pencil or two from the security guards?" said Honivi.

"Yes, we shall, right away." said Yekhalu.

The three seasoned soldiers then walked out of the jail wardroom as fresh learners and a teacher, on a mission to begin their schooling, and gathered enough materials, i.e. condensed milk wrappers and a few borrowed pencils from benevolent jail guards. Thus, a secret school for the Nagas in a jail ward of Nowgong Special Jail, Assam, had its birth.

Initially, they would borrow pencils and pens from the jail guards. Under the guidance of their comrade teacher, Sergeant Honivi, they would offer their breakfast slices of loaves to the guards and befriend them. Eventually, those policemen would smuggle in stationery for them.

"Besides offering them loaf slices, I would always sell off to the jail guards every packet of cigarettes (Panama Cigarette) we were issued. They, in return would buy me quires of papers, pencil and pen and at times, books even," narrated Yekhalu.

"Soon, many joined the classes. They were all so enthusiastic that most of them began reading English newspapers by the second year of jail schooling. Later on, a good number of them even earned certificates in Bible study through correspondence courses from different states of India, securing first division. They were all just great, not only as soldiers but students too. Had they an opportunity, some would have been a big officer in the government sectors back home and not a freedom fighter," narrates Sergeant Honivi Yeptho.

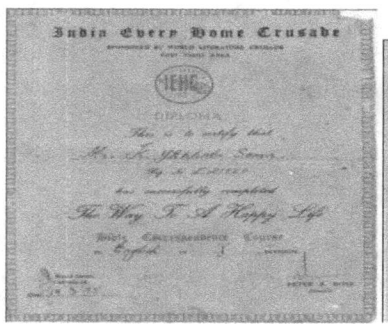
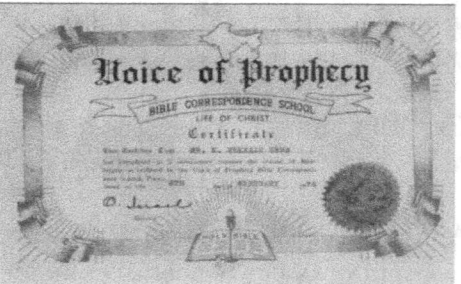
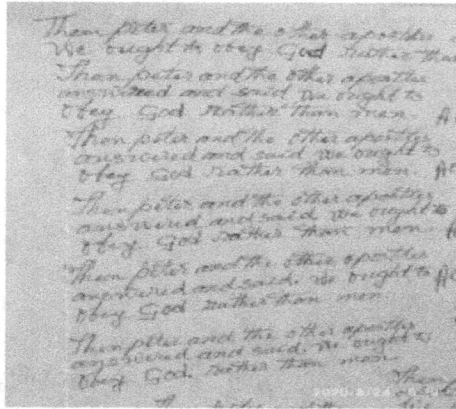
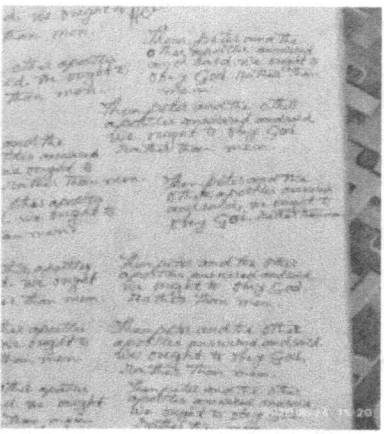

Correspondence course certificates and handwriting copies of Lieutenant Yekhalu Jimo, the man who never got to attend formal school but learnt from a friend in jail.

Later on, along with the teacher Honivi, Lieutenant Khukihe Shikhu also conducted Bible classes with an old coverless and unowned Holy Bible of the King James Version, found on a lonely shelf of Nowgong Special Jail library.

Being fairly impressed with the improvement of his comrade learners, Honrie Muivah, a Bachelor of Arts graduate, offered classes in English and Political Sciences in senior secondary courses to all that had attended fifth grade and above.

On 17th September, 1972, during the hearing for Criminal Revision No. 13 of 1970, the Guwahati High Court transferred the case to the court of Deputy Commissioner, Khasi Hills, Shillong. Consequently, a meeting between the Government of Nagaland and Chief Secretary Meghalaya, was held in the room of Chief Secretary, Meghalaya on 27th September, 1972. The implementation of the Guwahati High Court's order was discussed. Mr. T.C.K Lotha, Joint Secretary, Home; Er. Rynjah, Chief Engineer; Mr. P. Ahmed, Superintendent of Police, Kohima; and Mr Rai Barua, Architect, attended the meeting on behalf of the state of Nagaland.

In the meeting it was found that the existing Shillong jail was not in a position to hold those prisoners under trial, and therefore an alternative site at Mawlai was agreed by both governments. It was also agreed that all expenditure, such as construction of an additional jail, court premises, security forces, additional staff for the jail, incidental expenditure involved for the trial of the case, etc., will be reimbursed in full by the Government of Nagaland, but initially such expenditure will be met by the Government of Meghalaya.

The Government of Nagaland took up the matter with the Government of India, and the latter ultimately agreed to bear the expenses connected with the trial of the case. It also directed the Government of Nagaland to construct the court building, jail building, buildings for accommodating the police personnel and other constructed buildings at Mawlai. All these were completed within a record time of two months, and the jail was named Mawlai Special Jail, Shillong.

The Government of India also released three Battalions of Central Reserve Personnel to maintain law and order during the course of this trial, while Assam released an appropriate member of the jail staff for taking care of prisoners under trial at Mawlai. (Minutes of discussion held between Nagaland and Meghalaya government.)

Mawlai Special Jail, Shillong (1973-1976)

By March 17th 1973, they were transferred to Mawlai Special Jail, Shillong, a cool and a pleasant hilly town, the capital town of Meghalaya state; also known as the Scotland of the East.

The city, however cool and pleasant it may have been, did not make much difference to the Nagas who were kept behind the suffocating walls of Mawlai Special Jail. The hearts of many were as cold as the weather of the city, hardened by hatred against those who betrayed them into the enemy's hand and overwhelmed with the feelings of hatred and revenge. God, however, sent his servants to speak to these hardened hearts.

One day Rev. Shiwoto, Executive Secretary, Aizuto Centre of SBAK (Sumi Baptist Churches Association) visited the Naga inmates and shared God's Word with them, reading Bible passages from the books of Colossians and the Acts.

'Forbearing one another, and forgiving one another, if any man had a quarrel against any: even as Christ forgave you, so also do ye.' Colossian 3:13

'Repent ye therefore, and be converted that your sins may be blotted out, when the times of refreshing shall come from the presence of the Lord.' Acts 3:19

"My sons and brothers, you must make use of this time in jail to read the Bible daily. You must forgive one another, repent of your sins and come closer to God," said the Reverend, before he prayed for them and left.

After this, Rev. Kenneth Angami paid constant visits and had Sunday prayers with them. By the time Miss Beilieü Angami of Kohima and Rev. Musohi began visiting them, at least twenty Nagas were ready to get baptized. Therefore, though not the best, yet in the sweetest baptistery ever; in a trailer of an old jeep, the Nagas were baptized there in the premises of the jail.

Persecuted for a new-found faith

In the meantime, a staunch Seventh-day Adventist believer, Lieutenant Dr. Samson Luikham, with the help of his brother Y.D. Luikham, a Pastor of a Seventh-day Adventist Church who supplied the Bible materials, initiated a small Bible school by the name 'Bible School, Mawlai Special Jail' and offered a 'Seminar on Daniel and Revelation' to those willing.

Banner embroidered by Sergeant Honivi, 2nd Lieut. Yekhalu and Corporal Kharutsu.

It was attended by just seven of the Nagas; namely, Sergeant Honivi, the man who would translate Dr. Samson in his teachings, Captain Methani Chakesang, Lieutenant Yekhalu, Private Zuheto, Private Ghohevi, Private Qhuhoi and Zachive Chakesang; but Zachive was forcefully dragged away by his tribesmen and never allowed to attend the Bible classes.

At the end of a four-month seminar, Dr. Samson read out two passages, one from the Old, and the other from the New Testament of the Bible.

'Remember the Sabbath day, to keep it holy. Six days shalt thou labour and do all thy works: But the seventh day is the sabbath of the Lord thy God.' Exodus 20: 8-10

'And fear not them which kill the body, but are not able to kill the soul: but rather fear him which is able to destroy both soul and body in hell.'
Matthew 11: 28

The doctor earnestly exhorted them and said, "I have done my job, now it is up to you whether or not to choose the truth and the living God."

Yekhalu and Honivi being fairly convinced, instantly accepted the new faith and began worshipping with the doctor. Thus, the two men switched their faith from Baptism to Adventism, utterly unmindful of what awaited them for their new-found faith. The old comrades were not very happy with the duo for breaking away from Sunday worship as they all had been doing almost as their tradition ever since the Nagas converted to Christianity from Animism.

Initially they employed peaceful and verbal means to persuade the two to denounce the new faith. Corporal Kushokha Sumi, who declared and was believed by those men to have received three Spiritual trumpets from God during regular prayers conducted in the jail, began prophesying that Yekhalu should immediately denounce his new faith and re-join the old Baptist faith or face strong pain, and death ultimately. The man prophesied that a horn, like that of a rhinoceros would grow in Yekhalu's forehead within seven days should he not give up his faith and join the Baptist fold.

When this failed, the man prophesied again, that Yekhalu would soon have football sized abscess on his head. This too definitely failed.

The third time, the man said to Yekhalu, "God, despite your sins, has given you a last chance and this time, the Lord says, if you do not re-join your old faith, within seven days, you shall suffer an extremely severe fever and shall suffer loss of appetite and die a painful death within seven days."

"See, my friends, I bet you, I shall not even have a mere headache", confidently replied Lieutenant Yekhalu; and walked away from them.

On the seventh day after the last prophecy, Lieutenant Zhehoto Awomi rushed into Yekhalu's room and said, "Yekhalu, my friend, these men are all false prophets and I almost believed them. In fact, I have been observing you closely for all these days with an expectation to see all those things unfold in you, but they are wrong. So be resolute in your new faith. Initially, I believed that the prophecy would come true and I always visited my friend's room to see if he had a rhino-like horn in his forehead," narrated the man as he laughed at his own silliness.

The comrades that he once fought with were now ready to surprise him with many unexpected and awful activities against him. They would even mix the pork curry gravy with daal curry for Yekhalu and his Adventist friends to go hungry; but Yekhalu and his friend Honivi would ask for some chilli and salt from the cook and have it with plain rice mixed with water. Finally, perhaps out of frustration, those men even conspired against their officer and a comrade.

One Sunday afternoon, Private Pukhashe Sumi came calling for his commander Yekhalu. "Lieutenant, Sir, some of our Battalion men and other Sumi comrades have sent me to call you for a brief secret meeting," said the man, and walked out.

Yekhalu followed the Private, and as he entered the room filled with at least twenty of his Sumi comrades, he was given a rather uncomfortable welcome by those men that had gathered with a treacherous intention. Lance Corporal Ahoto stood up and began questioning the Lieutenant rather roughly and with not much respect. "'Where is your buddy Honivi? Is he not coming?" "I have no idea. I have come because I was told that we were having a meeting."

'So then, you mean to say you shall bear this for your friend too?" said the Lance Corporal and pushed his officer harshly. "Relax, buddy, tell me what the matter is and don't just push me like that," said the Lieutenant. "Then who, between you, said that those who eat pork, worship on Sunday and do not worship the Sabbath day shall perish?" angrily asked the man.

"Go ask the man who reported this to you, for I do what I believe is true and right. Also, of what you accuse, I am hearing it now and from you only," replied the Lieutenant calmly.

"So you mean to say you are the only righteous one?" fumed the man, and hit and injured the Lieutenant with a club that he kept hidden beneath his clothes.

Private Piwoto immediately rushed in and began to shout angrily. "Who organized this meeting?" fumed Private Piwoto. "Now listen up, everybody. I, Piwoto, son of Shihani of Ighanumi village, can by no means be a part of such a treacherous act as this. I shall go out and investigate it, and shall hold the man who instigated this act as guilty and responsible. You all are just a disgrace to the Nagas." said the Private and rushed out of the room. Soon, all the others followed the Private out and Yekahlu was left alone; free but injured and unattended.

Carried to the courts

The Nagas refused to attend any hearing of the courts so they were often forcefully dragged to the courts. During one such instance, the police and the security forces were made to carry them to the courtroom on stretchers and tarpaulin clothes. "Do not let your body hit or even touch the ground as they carry you. These rascals have no right to ill-treat us," Secretary Honrei Muivah advised the Naga comrades.

As they were being carried, Honrei Muivah intentionally rubbed his back on the ground and complained to the Superintendent, "Officer, your men are ill-treating me, you must tell them to be careful." "Careful with the men, you are aware of the consequences," scolded the superintendent.

When all were inside the courtroom, General Mowu, who was last carried in, shouted, "Nagaland for Christ." "Praise the Lord," shouted the Nagas. This happened for another two more times.

"Order, order, silence in the court," fumed the judge, as he banged his gavel. "Yes, it is no crime to praise the Lord. You may say it anywhere but the courtroom, and especially not in the manner you are doing it right now," continued the judge.

Once the court began to read out their names, the Nagas began praying and singing Church Hymnal songs that continued in a deafening sound till their names were read to the last. The judge finally had to adjourn the court for another date.

Refuse to sign the Shillong Accord

By November 11, 1975, Naga National Council/Federal Government of Nagaland had already signed the infamous Shillong Accord. Before long, some of its representatives visited the Nagas at Mawlai jail to persuade them to sign it. They were visited by Mr Kevi Yally, the signatory to the Accord and the younger brother of A.Z. Phizo, President of the NNC; Rev. Longri Ao, President Naga Peace Council and Member Liaison Committee, the body that played the role of Mediator for Shillong Accord; and Mr. Longshim Shaiza, Member of Liaison Committee.

A starving man, however strong his temperament may be, will most likely give in to their desire for food and water, for starving men seldom refuse the food that is offered to them. Leaders of the Federal Government of Nagaland and the Liaison Committee members had perhaps reposed their faith in their silly assumptions that those Naga Army soldiers must be yearning for release and, therefore, be susceptible to their treacherous plan. "Brave sons, you must be aware by now that the NNC/FGN has signed a Shillong Accord. You can set yourselves free only if you sign in support of the accord," persuaded those leaders.

"Many before us have perished. So shall we for the cause of Naga sovereignty, lest we forget those who have gone before us. We shall die here or at any other place or prison, but never shall we sign this treacherous accord," replied the Nagas, and rejected outright the only ticket to their lives.

At another time, Mr Ramuny, Advisor to the then Governor of Nagaland and Mr Dev, Commissioner Nagaland, also made an attempt, but failed to persuade these staunch Naga Freedom Fighters.

For seven years they were confined in three different jails, bludgeoned with clubs, tortured and placed under the heat of electric bulbs in cramped solitary cells on sweltering summer days, yet the brave Nagas squirmed not, nor did they give up their fight in exchange for their release, and yet the Nagas have forgotten these heroes who were betrayed and bartered off into the enemy's hand.

How could anyone who was so resolute even unto death for the liberty of his people be betrayed, rejected and forgotten by those he sacrificed his life for?

You're going home

On the morning of 7th May 1976, the Superintendent of Mawlai Special Jail, accompanied by the jailer and the assistant jailer, visited the Nagas with a surprise message that would leave them in total disbelief. "Men, you're going home tomorrow. Your respective district administrators have arrived to take you home. Pack all your belongings and be prepared to move out early tomorrow." Thus, the Naga Heroes were unconditionally allowed to walk out free from Mawlai Special Jail, Shillong, on the 8th May of 1976. Each of them was driven to their home by their respective Circle Officers.

2nd Lieutenant Zhehoto Awomi with tears in his sunken eyes choked, "As I happily rushed to my parents' home, a deserted and ruined wooden house gave me a cold and sad welcome. I had neither a home to stay in, nor a place to go. Both my parents had passed away and my brothers had migrated to another village."

As for Lance Corporal Kiyeto Sema, his courtyard bore no trees to have those 'yellow ribbons' tied around them and the house that held his family when he left for the Mission had fallen before the unfortunate blows of the cruel time.

"After I returned from Kachin land, I was captured and jailed at Zunheboto. When I was finally released from jail and reached home, my wife had become someone else's, and I had to build a new home with another lady," sadly recounted Lance Corporal Kiyeto Sema.

Lance Corporal Tokiye laments, "Calling my wife, as I raced home, a solitary widow in tears sallied out of that ramshackle house to receive me; but those tender ears of my wife were too far from receiving my cry; she had left my old mother alone, to live bereft and desolate in that half-broken home, doomed with love so untrue."

Those dwellings to them then became just empty houses without warmth. They were a home no more.

As Sergeant Honivi Yeptho happily walked down the narrow and grassy approach road towards his village, looking over at a couple working in a field above the road a few bends ahead, and wondering who the couple could be, he was taken by surprise to see his would-be father-in-law. "How are you, daddy?" Sergeant Honivi happily greeted the man.

Staring into the Sergeant's eyes intently, the astounded man cried out, "Honivi, my son, is that you? I never thought that I would ever see you again"

"Likewise, father dear," replied the Sergeant.

"My son, how can I even explain?" the man began to speak uneasily. "Your return proved almost impossible; her mother passed away and she could not bear the loss. Your fiancée has married someone else. Forgive us, son," said the man.

"It is okay, father dear, I hold none guilty but fate," helplessly replied Sergeant Honivi Yeptho, and walked up the lonely road empty-hearted.

Losing everything: their youth, their parents, their homes and their lovers to the cause of the Naga freedom; these brave and loyal men that fought for the Nagas are but now like a blind man in the morn, evoking the night's dream of his restored vision and whimpering a wistful wish to have been left unborn.

The bright eyes in the tired countenance of Lieutenant Yekhalu Jimo would sparkle in the reflections of the coursing tears every time he talks of the day he pattered down the old footpath of his village, Lizu Aviqato, below Zunheboto town.

"The house was soon thronged with all kinds of folks; young, old, women and children, and yet it felt so empty without the loving arms of my beloved parents to embrace me. My parents had been long gone; warm fire at the hearth of my house had long grown cold, and despite being in the company of many, I felt so lonesome," he lamented

From amongst the many, there was not his fiancée to be seen. Has the "No matter how long, you will find me here still waiting for you when we shall next meet," become a fanciful vow weathered by the storms of nine long years of wait?

"Yekhalu dear, your fiancée is now working as a government teacher at Timiwu Government Primary School.[3] We were made to believe that you shall never return, but now that you're back, my sister and you shall be together forever; we have sent her the message and she will be in the village soon," said the fiancée's brother. "Thank you, brother," calmly replied the Lieutenant.

When the fiancée returned from her posting place, a meeting between the two families was held at the brother's house one May afternoon, 1976. "My sister, the man you've waited for has finally returned; now tell us when we must get ready for the day," asked the fiancée's brother. The fiancée just looked down rather uncomfortably and remained strangely silent with no response. Yekhalu, sensing that something was not really right with his fiancée, interrupts. "My dear, I wish to speak to you in private. Can you meet me outside?"

She quietly followed him out of the door.

"My dear, what is this that I am sensing, what has gone wrong in my absence?" asked Yekhalu.

---

3 Fictitious name of the school used to conceal the identity of the fiancée.

"I cannot marry you," said the fiancée.

Yekhalu felt his heart miss a beat when he heard this. Nine years of bitter and painful experiences coupled with the flat denial from his lover boiled up inside him, but he managed to hold his emotions and calmly said:

"The officers and the government I loyally served have all betrayed me; both my parents are no more, I have none but you, please do not leave me, my dear." Lieutenant Yekhalu continued, "I have battled through these nine long bitter years with a strong hope that I shall be with you someday. When the days were bad, thoughts of you lightened my dark days. I already have a broken heart, as you are aware. Please do not hurt me. I may not be able to withstand another heartache."

The fiancée finally broke her silence and said, "I am sorry, dear, but I have already given away my heart to someone else and I cannot take it back, so please leave me and forget me."

The two lovers of the past silently entered the room where the family members were anxiously waiting to hear from them.

Yekhalu lowered his head for a moment, perhaps trying to conceal his tears; but as a brave soldier; mustered his courage, cleared his throat, lifted up his head and softly but boldly spoke out. "My brothers, sisters and family members, ask of her no more; she has waited enough. Nine years is long enough even for the woods to decay and this is not her fault; but it is my fate that God had already written for me. With shattered heart, I shall let her go and let her live her life as she pleases."

Then he turned towards the woman and said, "I have had a lot of people bid me goodbye and never have I wished them back because I hate goodbyes; but today I must wish you: Goodbye, dear."

Having wished her farewell, Lieutenant Yekhalu stepped out of the house and walked away, staring into the fading sun at the horizon, lost and dejected.

THE END

The Lost Mission

Lend an ear as I oblige thee, oh kind sir,
For the honour an old comrade thou offer.
If liberty erelong is attained and freedom regained,
I might truly desire to hold a post I've been trained.
But now this, a civil wing post I humbly must decline,
For I cannot govern with this poor command of mine.
Besides, why must an unqualified be preferred
While leaving the deserving rejected and unheard?
No sir, you must to my plea hearken this time
For to hold an office sans proficiency is a crime.

The gentleman seated across your table insisted
That his father to the veterans' list must be enlisted,
Perhaps he doesn't remember what we've once done.
We chose death for liberty of our people. "My son,"
Said I, "I don't care if heaven for me is pulled down
And the earthly glory and fame be my crown,
E'en if stacks of the package-gotten bills reach the sky,
Ne'er shall associate with men that causes liberty to die
And betrays the blood of heroes shed for Naga liberty.
Wealth through betrayal? Nay, I shall choose poverty."

Tears of widows, orphans and parents of the slain
And many a thousand soldiers' blood, tears and pain,
Like Abel's, surely must have cried out to heaven.
How then shall I face them, if that realm I enter fallen.
And now as my day draweth closer to sunset, why must
I bow before treasures obtained through ways unjust?
We have once in the hands of a brother lost a mission,
Under no circumstances do I wish to see a repetition.
Sir, remember? When from the Mission we arrived,
We both thought that the ordeal we had survived.

Nay, it wasn't for hatred they took a deceitful action;
'Twas for the benefit of Nagas they formed a new faction
And when into that trusted camp the Captain guided us in,
Came Judaistic kisses and hugs from true leaders therein.
And perhaps to the unlucky Captain unbeknown,
Those loyal leaders had conspired against their own.
Violence they loathed, so in an attempt to save our breath,
They happily helped the enemy to punish us with death.
Oh, what joy the fallen leaders must have felt when
Our lives they saved into the foe's hands; their friends then.

No Sir, it wasn't that either, why have us martyred
Just for a petty fortune? We were simply bartered.
Oh, how pure and selfless leaders were they
That for freedom's sake huge riches amassed away,
And take pride in their acts singing songs
Of innocence and praises for their wrongs.
Hitherto, to the people, stainless they may have stayed
But a whited sepulchre has history have them portrayed.
Truly unlike them you are, wherefore you command my respect
But should you too bow down, support from us never expect.

If for a package to settle, why struggle these many years;
If to become one of them, why after too much blood and tears
Have been shed? Why must we be forced into submission?
Why must the posterity mock it as the Lost Mission?
Would Sir please convey to his Excellency Yaruiwo the message
And tell him also that liberty alone shall be our heritage.
Kilonser Sir, Yes, once a senior officer I was but now it is fair
To address you Sir and not friend, in honour of your chair.
May your fight for liberty soon come to fruition
As we patiently await; may it never become the Lost Mission.

Pekingto Y. Jimo

Postscript

While it is true that the Nagas were incomparable to a nation as mighty as India, yet, the Nagas were like a speck in her eyes and gave its leaders many gruelling nights. The undivided Naga forces that fought for Naga sovereignty tormented India enough like a thorn in the flesh.

Yesterday, we fought India in extreme bravery and India certainly felt the strength and courage of the Nagas; but she soon managed to spot the Achilles' heel of the Nagas. India discovered that many of the Naga leaders were selfish and that is the reason why we are fighting her agents in our own backyard today. Tomorrow, we shall not be fighting India, we shall rather be fighting our own brothers and the blood spilt shall be our own.

"India tactfully separated the RGN from FGN. Once, a high-ranking Indian Army officer made an offer. He promised to provide rations and all forms of logistic support if I were to form a new faction," said Col. J P Vikugha. The aid and such other supports that the Government of India offers for every new faction is nothing but a ploy to further disintegrate the Naga people, and to paralyze its fight for freedom.

We have wrongly assumed that tribalism and disunity have destroyed the spirit of Naga nationalism. Rather, it was selfishness that fostered the two factors to destroy the Nagas. Selfishness causes disunity and disunity gradually leads to disintegration. This is what happened to Naga nationalism. It is neither the Nagas from the south nor the Nagas from the central, but selfishness of some Nagas that has shattered the Nagas' dream of a free and sovereign Naga land. It was sheer selfishness that caused the split that disintegrated the great NNC/FGN. It was selfishness that killed many Naga patriots including Mr. Kuhovi Jimomi, Kilonser of Rali Wali, Federal Government of Nagaland, who was captured and mercilessly bayoneted to death by the agents of the enemy on 1st December, 1973.

Nagas have had enough of a running battle with India. Every Naga, irrespective of tribe and strength, has contributed to the fight; but we have also had enough of battles within ourselves in the form of disunity, fear, corruption, fratricide and hatred against each other. If we still continue to carry that hatred today, we are worse than those who have mowed down the Nagas' aspirations to nothing but dust and ashes.

Nagas have bitterly fought for Independence and sovereignty, but in the process we have perhaps locked ourselves into a losing battle. We may have fought a futile war. We may have lost the Mission and might as well see it happen time and again if we continue seeking liberty under such a massively divided house.

It is time for the Nagas to wake up from slumber, and move forward in love, peace and unity.

The Veterans Who Told Their Story

Captain Sanguto Chase
4th Battalion, 2nd Brigade
1st Division, Southern Command
Naga Army

Captain Sakole Yokha
5th Battalion, 2nd Brigade
1st Division, Southern Command
Naga Army
(The same Jacket he had worn when he was injured)

Lieutenant Dr. Samson Luikham,
7th Battalion, 3rd Brigade
1st Division, Southern Command.
Naga Army.

2nd Lieutenant Yekhalu Jimo
Naga Army No. 1832, 14th Battalion, 24 Coy,
5th Brigade, 2nd Division
Central Command, Naga Army.

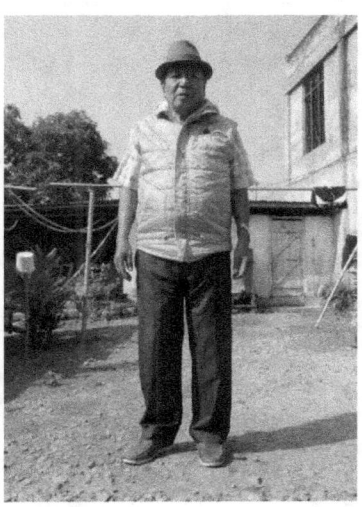

2nd Lieutenant Rowndar Anal,
7th Battalion,
3rd Brigade, 1st Division,
Southern Command.
Naga Army.

2nd Lieutenant K. Zhehoto Awomi
Naga Army No. 4266,
11th Battalion,
4th Brigade, 2nd Division
Central Command, Naga Army

2nd Lieutenant Lhousinyu Angami
6th Battalion, 2nd Brigade
1st Division, Southern Command
Naga Army

Sergeant Major Krutsolie Ziru
6th Battalion, 2nd Brigade
1st Division, Southern Command
Naga Army

Sergeant Honivi Yeptho
Naga Army No. 4742, 4th Brigade Staff
2nd Division, Central Command,
Naga Army.

Sergeant Renthungo Odyuo
17th Battalion, 6th Brigade.
2nd Division, Central Command,
Naga army

Sergeant Tokim Tikhir,
4th Bde Staff, Central Command, Naga Army

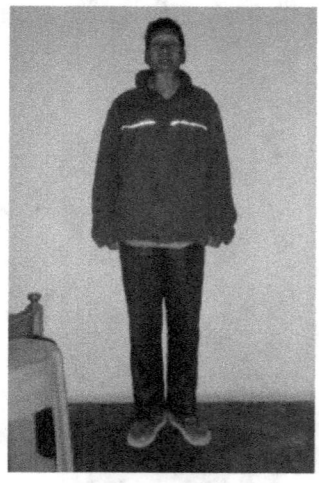

Sergeant Samatai Luikham
7th Battalion, 3rd Brigade
1st Division, Southern Command.
Naga Army.

Sergeant S. Pitu Jourü
10th battallion, 4th Brigade, Central Command, Naga Army.

Corporal Pukhato Swu
14th Battalion, 5th Brigade
2nd Division, Central Command,
Naga Army.

Corporal Khamkhui Tangkhul
7th Battalion, 3rd Brigade
1st Division, Southern Command.
Naga Army.

Corporal Kahie Angami
4th Battalion, 2nd Brigade
1st Division, Southern Command
Naga Army

Lance Corporal Kiyeto Sema
12th Battalion, 4th Brigade, 2nd Division
Central Command, Naga Army

Lance Corporal Tokiye Wotsa
Naga Army No. 4653, 12th Battalion,
4th Brigade, 2nd Division
Central Command, Naga Army

Private Shutümi Jorror.
10 battallion, 4 Brigade, Central Command, Naga Army

Private Rüzhükhrie Kense
6th Battalion, 2rd Brigade
1st Division, Southern Command
Naga Army.

Private Resieto Kense
6th Battalion, 2nd Brigade
1st Division, Southern Command
Naga Army.

Private Visiekhrie Kense
6th Battalion, 2nd Brigade
1st Division, Southern Command
Naga Army.

Private Sailanbo Liangmai
4th Battalion, 2nd Brigade
1st Division, Southern Command
Naga Army.

Private Shürhitso Metha
6th Battalion, 2nd Brigade
1st Division, Southern Command
Naga Army.

Private Zuheto Chishi
Naga Army No. 4449, 12th Battalion
4th Brigade, 2nd Division
Central Command, Naga Army

Private Yehaxe Sumi
14th Battalion, 5th Brigade
2nd Division, Central Command,
Naga Army.

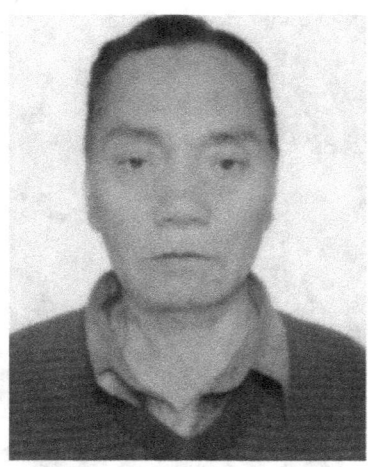

Pte. Heshito Sumi
12th Battalion
4th Brigade, 2nd Division
Central Command, Naga Army

Private Vihoqhe Sumi
4th Brigade Staff, 2nd Division
Central Command, Naga Army

Private Salumo Sheqhi
14th Battalion, 5th Brigade
2nd Division, Central Command,
Naga Army.

Pte. Ghujuhe Futhena
14th Battalion, 5th Brigade,
Central Command , Naga Army.

Private Kichotsing Sangtam 11th Battalion,
4th Brigade, 2nd Division
Central Command, Naga Army

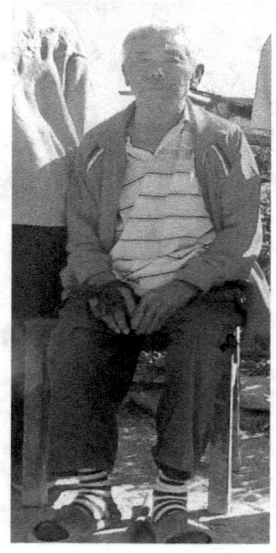

Private Heshena Assumi
14th Battalion, 5th Brigade
2nd Division, Central Command,
Naga Army.

Private Kivito Achumi
14th Battalion, 5th Brigade
2nd Division, Central Command,
Naga Army.

Private Lhoxuto Assumi
14th Battalion, 5th Brigade
2nd Division, Central Command,
Naga Army.

Private Pukhalu (Akhalu) Assumi
14th Battalion, 5th Brigade
2nd Division, Central Command,
Naga Army.

Private Ivulho Lohe
14th Battalion, 5th Brigade
2nd Division, Central Command,
Naga Army.

Private Soleo Piele
6th Battalion, 2nd Brigade
1st Division, Southern Command
Naga Army.

Private Pheluolhou Chase
6th Battalion, 2nd Brigade
1st Division, Southern Command
Naga Army.

Pte. Piwoto Sumi
14th Battallion, 5th Brigade, 2nd Division,
Central Command, Naga Army.

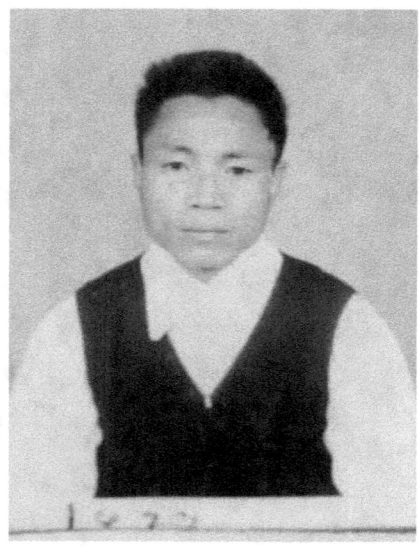

Captain Kochu Pochury
4 Brigade Staff, Central Command,
Naga Army.

Left –right.
(i)Th. Muivah, (ii) Brig. Nidiliu Angami, (iii) Chekhuve Chakesang, (iv) Corporal Visazo Angami. (v) Pte. Visiekhrie Kense, (vi) L/Corpl. Kiyeto Sema, (vii) Capt. Atong Zeliang. (Photographed by Gen. Thinosilie at International House, Kunming, China.)

Standing: L-R. Sergeant Honivi Yeptho, 2nd Lieutenant Yekhalu Jimo, Private Zuheto Chishi
Seating: L-R. 2nd Lieutenant Zhehoto Awomi, Asu Isak Chishi Swu, Mrs. Euster Chishi Swu, Sergeant Jehoto Sumi.

Appendix I The Command Enrolment

Group A. Central Command

1. Isak Chishi Swu of Chishilimi, Foreign Secretary, NNC/FGN and President's Special Envoy to China
2. Raju Peyu Vihoshe Shohe of Vekuho,
3. Mr. Vihei Swu of Khekiye

4/ Brigade Staff. 52 Naga Army, 10 Action Rifle with 550 rounds, one Stengun with 60 rounds. Command certificate issued by Brigadier I. Kivihe Swu, Commander, 4th Brigade.

1. Captain Yeshiho Sumi of Surumi, 4/Bde staff unit commander
2. Captain Kochu Pochury of Yesimi
3. Captain Tsupichu Pochury of Phor, Unit QM. Incharge
4. Sergeant Major Luvishe Sumi of Surumi, unit Sergeant Major
5. Sergeant Honivi Sumi of Melahumi, unit office clerk
6. Sergeant Tokim Tikhir of Pokphur
7. L/Corporal Thongtsi Tikhir of Chikipongru
8. L/Corporal Khenchumong Tikhir of Shamutor
9. L/Corporal Heqhezu Sumi of Sutimi
10. L/Corporal Kiusumong Tikhir of Pokphur
11. L/Corporal Tohevi Tikhir of Chikipongru
12. L/Corporal Yenchu Tikhir of Sangkhumti
13. L/Corporal Khentsu Tikhi of Waphor
14. L/Corporal Risumong Tikhir of Chomi
15. Pte. Khulimthong Tikhir of Chikipongru
16. Pte. Chimthong Tikhir of Chikipongru
17. Pte. Thongthong Tikhir of Chikipongru
18. Pte. Yamlu Tikhir of Chikipingru
19. Pte. Tsamong Tikhir of Mütungrü
20. Pte. Tothung Tikhir of Mütungrü
21. Pte. Khiungakiu Tikhir of Sangkhumti
22. Pte. Shumong Tikhir of Sangkhumti
23. Pte. Risumong Tikhir of Thonoknyu
24. Pte. Khentsu Tikhir of Thonoknyu
25. Pte. Thongthong Tikhir of Shamator
26. Pte. Phanongthong TIkhir of Shamator

27. Pte. Phanongkiu Tikhir of Shamator
28. Pte. Limtsu Tikhir of Waphor
29. Pte. Khiumong Tikhir of Waphor
30. Pte. Tothung Tikhir of Waphor
31. Pte. Richungkiu Tikhir of Waphor
32. Pte. Pinsolim Tikhir of Anadangrü
33. Pte. Tsamong Tikhir of Anadangrü
34. Pte. Tsumongthong Tikhir of Anadangrü
35. Pte. Khiungmong Tikhir of Anadangrü
36. Pte. Khiungakiu Tikhir of Anadangrü
37. Pte. Tsinthong Tikhir of Anadangrü
38. Pte. Ahuse Tikhir of Pungro
39. Pte. Yutsumong Tikhir of Chomi
40. Pte. Yongpenthomng Tikhir of Chomi
41. Pte. Iqheto Sumi of Sukimi
42. Pte. Vihokhe Sumi of Sukimi
43. Pte. Vihekhu Sumi of Sukimi
44. Pte. Vighozu Sumi of Sukimi
45. Pte. Yenshumong Tikhir of Suki A
46. Pte. Vitoshe Sumi of Saghemi
47. Pte. Limidimong Tikhir of Shamator
48. Pte. Pashi Tikhir of Chiliso
49. Pte. Chiu Tikhir of Chiliso
50. Pte. Yamukam Tikhir of Sangkhumti
51. Pte. Chimthong Tikhir of Chikipongru
52. Pte. Toripkiu Tikhir of Mütungrü

10th Battalion 14 Naga Army, 7 Rifles with 385 rounds, Command Certificate issued by Lieutenant Colonel Henito Sumi.

1. Lieut. Nyukhapa Pochury of Melury, unit Commander
2. Sergeant Major Chükhüra Pochury of Phokhungri,
3. Sergeant Major Laxheje Sumi of Shoixe, unit Sergt. Major
4. Sergeant Chepong Pochury of Sütsü unit QM in charge
5. Sergeant S. Pitu Jourü of Phor village
6. Corporal Karutsu Pochury of Sütsü, unit clerk
7. Pte. Ritatu Pochury of Phor village
8. Pte. Shutümi Pochury of Phor village
9. Pte. Thüleytsü Pochury of Phokhungri village

10. Pte. Chitatu Pochury of Sütsü village
11. Pte. Losang Pochury of Sütsü village
12. Pte. Yungpenthong Pochury of Mukhor
13. Pte. Yutsumong Pochury of Moya
14. Pte. Zupongtsu Pochury of Sütsü

11ᵗʰ Battalion; 29 Naga Army, one Light Machine Gun, 7 Rifles with 485 rounds, one 2 inch mortar with five shells. Command certificate issued by Lieutenant Colonel Zukiye Jimo

1. Captain Itokhu Sumi of Luvishe village
2. 2/ Lieut. Jehoto Sumi of Lukhami, unit Commander
3. 2/Lieut. Khukihe Sumi of Sutimi, PS.to Isak Chishi Swu
4. Sgt.Major Kivije Sangtam of Natsami, unit Sgt.Major
5. Sgt. Ihoshe Sumi of Thakiye,
6. Corporal Nihozu Sumi of Tsukomi, unit clerk
7. Corporal Zuheto Sumi of Lukhami,
8. Corporal Suhoi Sumi of Thazuvi, Unit QM in charge
9. L/Corporal Tsangkhuchu Samphury of Langturü village
10. Pte. Luapongchu Samphury of Langturü village
11. Pte. Mlayi Samphury of Langturü village
12. Pte. Seksenthe Samphury of Longkha village
13. Pte. Intsochu Samphury of Longmatra village
14. Pte. Kichotsing Sangtam of Natsami village
15. Pte. Tsoingki Samphury of Langturü village.
16. Pte. Qhewoto Sumi of Sutimi village
17. Pte. Litsamong Sangtam of Yethsumi village
18. Pte. Zukhuvi Sumi of Shothu village
19. Pte. Luashemung Samphury of Lamrorü village
20. Pte. Thuliki Samphury of Lamrorü village
21. Pte. Yamusu Samphury of Langturü village
22. Pte. Ghohevi Sumi of Sutimi village
23. Pte. Tungathe Samphury of Longkha village
24. Pte. Tsathenki Samphury of Longkha village
25. Pte. Thrumuso Samphury of Longkha village
26. Pte. Tsangkimung Samphury of Longkha village
27. Pte. Nijeto Sumi of Phisami village
28. Pte. Sepenthe Samphury of Langturü village
29. Pte. Yangsemong Sangtam of Kisetung village

12/Battalion, 29 Naga Army, one Light-Machine-Gun, 20 Rifles with 1150 rounds, Command certificate issued by Lieutenant Colonel Honije Sumi.

1. Sgt. Shikuto Sumi of Kiyekhu, unit Commander
2. Sgt. Jehoto Sumi of Thsuruhumi, unit Sgt.Major
3. Corp. Tsawoto Sumi of Thakiye village
4. Corp. Yehoto Sumi of Xukhepu, unit clerk
5. Corporal Ghohuto Sumi of Jekiye, unit QM. In charge
6. Corp. Latoje Sumi of Kiyekhu village
7. Corp. Nahevi Sumi of Thakiye village
8. Corp. Qhujeto Sumi of Kivukhu village
9. L/Corp. Kiyeto Sumi of Sheipu village
10. L/Corp. Tokiye Sumi of Achikuchu village
11. L/Corp. Shiqhei Sumi of Thazuvi village
12. L/Corp, Luvishe Sumi of Saghemi village
13. Pte. Zuheto Sumi of Luthsumi village
14. Pte. Yeqhevi Sumi of Phulesheto village
15. Pte. Vixeshe Sumi of Kathara village
16. Pte. Xetoi Sumi of Lukhuyi village
17. Pte. Heshito Sumi of Khulhopu village
18. Pte. Zuhei Sumi of Thakiye village
19. Pte. Qhuhoi Sumi of Tsutoho village
20. Pte. Tojevi Sumi of Ghokhuvi village
21. Pte. Vihuto Sumi of Qhekiye village
22. Pte. Lutovi Sumi of Khukishe village
23. Pte. Jenihe Sumi of Khukishe village
24. Pte. Tokiho Sumi of Nihoshe village
25. Pte. Yetoje Sumi of Sukhalu village
26. Pte. Vitoje Sumi of Sheipu village
27. Pte. Niqhekhu of Lochhomi village
28. Pte. Inuvi Sumi of Surumi village
29. Pte. Hekiye Sumi of Vedami village

14/Battalion, 38 Naga Army, one Light Machine Gun, 18 Rifles with 925 rounds, Command Certificate issued by Lieutenant Colonel Salumo Sumi

1. 2/ Lieut.Yekhalu Sumi of Lizumi, Unit Commander
2. 2/Lieut.Yetovi Sumi of Usutomi village, unit 2 I/C
3. Sgt. Major Inavi Sumi of Mukalimi, unit Sergt. Major

4. Sgt. Nihokhu Sumi of Chishilimi,
5. Corporal Kushokha Sumi of Ighanu village
6. Corporal Akhalu Shikhu of Lazami village,
7. Corporal Pukhato Sumi of Shesulimi, unit QM. In charge
8. Lance Corporal Satoi Sumi of Ghokimi village
9. Lance Corporal Ahoto Sumi of Mishilimi village
10. Pte. Piwoto Sumi of Ghokimi village
11. Pte. Khunito Sumi of Chishilimi village
12. Pte. Piwoto Sumi of Ighanumi, unit clerk
13. Pte. Yehaxe Sumi of Kichilimi village
14. Pte. Lhoxuto Sumi of Kichilimi village
15. Pte. Jevishe Sumi of Tsaphimi village
16. Pte. Kivito Achumi of Natsumi, village
17. Pte. Heshena Sumi of Natsumi village
18. Pte. Pukhalu Sumi (Akhalu) of Natsumi village
19. Pte. Salumo Sumi of Mishilimi village
20. Pte. Ghujukha Sumi of Mishilimi village
21. Pte. Ivulho Sumi of Lazami village
22. Pte. Heshito Sumi of Lazami village
23. Pte. Ghujuhe Sumi of Lazami village
24. Pte. Ghujuhe Eyenu of Lazami village
25. Pte. Khumtsa Sumi of Lazami village
26. Pte. Xukiye Sumi of Iphonumi village
27. Pte. Vikiye Sumi of Iphonumi village
28. Pte. Pukhalu Sumi of Ighanumi village
29. Pte. Akhalu Sumi of Ighanu village
30. Pte. Jikhato Sumi of Ighanu village
31. Pte. Inavi Sumi of Ighanu village
32. Pte. Pukhashe Sumi of Hebolimi village
33. Pte. Kughato Sumi of Hebolimi village
34. Pte. Ghilesho Sumi of Hebolimi village
35. Pte. Avito Sumi of Ighanumi village.
36. Pte. Woipu of Tsaphimi
37. Pte. Ghilikha of Mishilimi village
38. Pte. Sheniyie of Ighanumi

Five Naga Army from **16th and 17th Battalion,** of 6/Bde came along C-in-C, General Mowu Gwizantsu. Since they belonged to the Central Command and less in number so they were attached to the 14th Battalion. Rifle 2 with 110 rounds.

1. Sergeant Renthungo Lotha of Yikhum village, 17th Battalion
2. Corporal N-Nungrhomo Lotha of Akok village, 16th Battalion
3. Pte. Nchupomo Lotha of Changsu old, 17th Battalion
4. Pte. Nchipemo Lotha of Riphyim Old, 17th Battalion
5. Pte. Nzanpemo Lotha of Mekokla village, 17th Battalion

Group B Southern Command,
150 Naga Army, the group was divided into two Companies, A Coy and B Coy. A Coy Commander Captain Sakolie Yokha and B Coy Commander Captain Lhounizo of Rosoma.

4/Battalion,
1. General Mowu Gwizantsu Angami of Khonoma
2. Captain Sanguto Chase of Khonoma
3. Lieutenant Megosazo Chase of Khonoma
4. Lieut. Kokhoto Vakha Angami of Khonoma
5. 2/Lieut. Nirazha-o Angami of Ruzama
6. 2/Lieut. Nisa Vupru Angami of Khonoma
7. S/Major Mhidu-u Angami of Viphoma
8. S/Major Vitsolie Angami of Jotsoma
9. S/Major Akhou-u Angami of Khonoma
10. S/Major Theyiejuhie Angami of Khonoma
11. S/Major Lhusakhonyü Angami of Jotsoma
12. Sgt. Thepfuselhou Angami of Mezoma
13. Sgt. Ketsohu Angami of Mengujuma
14. Corporal Kahie Angami of Vephoma
15. Corp. Pfülhouvi Angami of Sechüma
16. Pte. Thejayagwi Angami of Kiruphema
17. Pte. Mhiesilie Angami of Khonoma
18. Pte. Khoto Dolie Angami of Khonoma
19. Pte. Rüyahulie Angami of Khonoma,
20. Pte. Rulie Angami of Khonoma
21. Pte. Rukhrehie Mor Angami of Khonoma
22. Pte. Nichumelie Angami of Khonoma
23. Pte. Nithongulie Angami of Khonoma
24. Pte. Rajuvito Angami of Thekrejuma
25. Pte. Pfuvito Angami of Jotsoma
26. Pte. Zeluolie Angami of Jotsoma

27. Pte. Sasieto Angami of Jotsoma
28. Pte. Khrienyuphe-u Angami of Mezoma
29. Pte. Viyiezo Angami of Jotsoma
30. Pte. Keviavie Angami of Rüzaphema
31. Pte. Letuo Angami of Ruzaphema,
32. Pte. Salambo Liangmei of Intuma
33. Pte. Athimbo LiangmeiofIntuma
34. Pte. Nisakhoto Angami of Khonoma
35. Pte. Kichugwelhou Angami of Ruzama

From 5th Battalion
1. Colonel Lhouvicha Angami of Pfüchama
2. Captain Sakole Yokha of Kigwema
3. Captain Kehokri Angami of Kidima
4. 2/Lieut. Kaito Angami of Kidima
5. Sgt. Zhosal Angami of Viswema
6. Sgt. Dikho Zutso of Kigwema
7. Corporal Visazo Belho of Kigwema
8. Corporal Maga Angami of Viswema
9. Chaplain Vichaneio Angami of Mima
10. Pte. Sieto Thorie of Kigwema
11. Pte. Siesa Thorie of Kigwema
12. Pte. Thinolhou Yhoshü of Kigwema
13. Pte. Neikhrielie Kire of Kigwema
14. Pte. Theyievi Angami of Kigwema
15. Pte. Kedisa Sale of Kigwema
16. Pte. Zelolie Zashumo of Phesama
17. Pte. NinguzolieTacu of Phesama
18. Pte. Ngusa Peki Angami of Mima
19. Pte. Banyu Angami of Mima
20. Pte. Kelhouyasa Peki Angami of Mima
21. Pte. Pupa Lese Angami of Mima,
22. Pte. Pfutso Angami of Mima
23. Pte. Sato Angami of Jakhama
24. Pte. Savil Angami of Viswema
25. Pte. Punil Angami of Khuzama
26. Pte. Kezevihol Angami of Khuzama
27. Pte. Zadel Angami of Khuzama
28. Pte. Esol Angami of Khuzama,

29. Pte. Khrulvi Angami of Kidima
30. Pte. Nasal Angami of Kidima
31. Pte. Kerisa Angami of Kidima
32. Pte. Kenihosa Angami of Kidima,
33. Pte. Visizol (Tehibu) Angami of Kidima,
34. Pte. Tsonoho Angami of Kezoma
35. Pte. Yodi Kintso of Kidima
36. Pte. Yopi Angami of Kezoma
37. Pte. Nothul Angami of Chakhabama
38. Pte. Pungusa Angami of Chakhabama
39. Pte. Kehovicho Angami of Chakhabama

From 6th Battalion
1. Captain Neila-o Angami of Kohima
2. Captain Guovilie Angami of Nerhema
3. Captain Lhounizo Angami of Rüsoma
4. 2/Lieut. Mesevi Angami of Nerhema
5. 2/Lieut. Lhousinyu Angami of Nerhema
6. 2/Lieut. Khrielakuo Angami of Kohima
7. Sgt. Major Khe-o Angami of Kohima
8. Sgt. Major Ketoulhoulie (Azie) Angami of Kohima,
9. Sgt. Major Krutsolie Angami of Tuophema
10. S/Major Lhoupfelie Angami of Rüsoma
11. Sgt. Khrietso Angami of Chiedema
12. Sgt. Neitsuhu Angami of Nerhema
13. Sgt. Viselhou Angami of Dihoma
14. Corporal Sobunuo Angami of Kohima
15. Corporal Mezhüzolie Angami of Kohima
16. Corporal Vizotuo Angami of Kohima
17. Corporal Lhe-o Angami of Kohima
18. Corporal Azei Angami of Kohima
19. Corporal Vitsolie Angami of Tuophema
20. Corporal Luozilie Angami of Tuophema
21. Corporal Yasie-o Angami of Tuophema
22. Corporal Lhoutsonyü Angami of Zhadima
23. Corporal Thinuovilie Angami of Zhadima
24. Corporal Kiyewhelie Angami of Phekerükriema,
25. Corporal Kelhoulezo Angami of Rusoma
26. L/Corporal Suolahie Angami of Kohima

27. Pte. Zalhoupra Angami of Kohima
28. Pte. Ketoulhoulie Angami of Kohima
29. Pte. Viyieselie Angami of Kohima
30. Pte. Vibunuo Angami of Kohima
31. Pte. Neisielie Angami of Kohima
32. Pte. Khriezei-o Angami of Kohima
33. Pte. Sale Angami of Kohima
34. Pte. Seikuolie Angami of Kohima
35. Pte. Rüzhükhrie Kense of Tuophema
36. Pte. Visiekhrie Angami of Tuophema
37. Pte. Resietso Angami of Tuophema
38. Pte. Kethoneilhou Angami of Tuophema
39. Pte. Pusimo Angami of Tuophema
40. Pte. Vitsomo Angami of Tuophema
41. Pte. Tsoselie Angami of Tuophema
42. Pte. Tholie Angami of Tuophema
43. Pte. Rüülhou Angami of Chiechama
44. Pte. Chavi Angami of Chiechama
45. Pte. Shusilie Angami of Chiechama
46. Pte. Tsao Angami of Chiechama
47. Pte. Souchulie Angami of Chiechama
48. Pte. Zeneipra Angami of Chiechama
49. Pte. Vo-o Angami of Tichüma
50. Pte. Zuuzelie Angami of Zhadima
51. Pte. Diethonyu Angami of Zhadima
52. Pte. Pelhoutsu Angami of Dihoma
53. Pte. Thinuoselhou Angami of Rusoma
54. Pte. Teisovilhou Angami of Kijumetouma
55. Pte. Soleo Angami of Gariphema
56. Pte. Pheluolhou Chase of Gariphema
57. Pte. Dziesengulie Angami of Gareiphema
58. Pte. Zapra-o Angami of Chiechama
59. Pte. Pfucha Angami of Kohima,
60. Pte. Shürhitso Metha of Chiechema

From 7th Battalion
1. Lieut. Ngairem Phungshok Tangkhul of Somdal
2. Lieut. Doctor Samson Luikham Tangkhul of Ukhrul
3. 2/Lieut. Compounder A.R. Aso Tangkhul of Ukhrul,

4. 2/Lieut. Rownder Anal of Tengnopal
5. 2/Lieut. Khayapshai Shimray Tangkhul of Tuinem
6. Secretary Honrei Muivah Tangkhul of Ngaigai PS.to C.in C.
7. LM. Sanyi Mao of Tonjoy, Publicity Secretary
8. Sergeant Samatai Tangkhul of Ukhrul
9. Sergeant Dharma Singh Meitei of Imphal
10. Corporal Khamkhui Tangkhul of Lampui (Ramva)
11. Pte. Adani Mao of Tonjoy
12. Pte. Vareichin Tangkhul of Ukhrul
13. Pte. Wonmi Tangkhul of Somdal
14. Pte. Maiphai Tangkhul of Sinailong
15. Pte. Theingairio Tangkhul of Phulung
16. Pte. Kayangnam Tangkhul of Phulung

Appendix II

Heroes Fallen in the Mission.

1. Private Mhalevo of Chiechama Village, 6th Battalion, 2nd Brigade, Southern Command, Naga Army. Drowned at Tizü River, Nagaland, on December 8, 1967.
2. Private Tsumongthong Tikhir of Anadangru village, 10th Battalion, 4th Bde Staff, Central Command, Naga Army. Lost in Ngalang dense forest on 9th January, 1968
3. Private Khumtsa of Lazami Village, 14th Battalion, 5th Brigade, Central Command, Naga Army. Died at Ngalang Taung Mountain in Sagaing region Myanmar on January 11, 1968.
4. Private Neisielie Angami of Kohima village, 5th Battalion, 2 Bde, Southern Command Naga Army. Left at KIA camp due to illness and never returned.
5. Private Thongthong Tikhir of Chikipongru village, 4th Brigade staff, Central Command Naga Army. Died on 15th June, 1968 at Baoshan Hospital, China.
6. Private Rüyahulie Seyie aka Yahu son of Ngulhuto Seyie of Khonoma village, 4th Battalion 2nd Brigade, Southern Command, Naga Army. Drowned at N'Mai Hka River, in Kachin land, Burma on November 18, 1968.
7. Sergeant Major Chükhüra Pochury of Phokhungri village, 10th Battalion, 4th Brigade, Central Command, Naga Army. Killed in action at Nchunglova Yang a Kachin village on 22nd November, 1968.
8. Corporal N-Nungrhomo Lotha of Akok village, 16th Battalion, 6 Bde, Central Command, Naga Army. Killed in action at Nchunglova Yang, a Kachin village on 22nd November, 1968.
9. Lance Corporal Heqhezu Sumi of Sutimi, 4th Bde Staff, Central Command, Naga Army. Killed in action at Nchunglova Yang, a Kachin village on 22nd November, 1968.
10. Sergeant Shikuto Sumi of Kiyekhu village, 12th Battalion, Central Command, Naga Army. Succumbed to injury sustained at Nchunglova Yang a Kachin village on 22nd November, 1968.

11. Sergeant Major Ketoulhoulie aka Azie, son of Menyieo of Kohima Village 6th Battalion, 2nd Brigade, Southern Command, Naga Army. Killed in action near Gumshen village in kachin land on 27th December, 1968.
12. Corporal Mezhüzolie, son of Kuolievi of Kohima village, 6th Battalion, 2nd Brigade Southern Command, Naga Army. Killed in action near Gumshen village in kachin land on 27th December, 1968.
13. Private Zhalhoupra, son of Lhoupulie of Kohima village, 6th Battalion, 2nd Brigade Southern Command, Naga Army. Killed in action near Gumshen village in kachin land on 27th December, 1968.
14. 2nd Lieutenant A.R. Aso Tangkhul of Ukhrul Manipur, 7th Battalion, 3rd Brigade Southern Command, Naga Army. Killed in action near Ngakhet village in kachin land on 27th December, 1968.
15. Private Khiungmong Tikhir of Anadangrü village, 4th brigade staff, Central Command, Naga Army. Killed in action at Putao road on 3rd December, 1968.
16. Private Woipu Sumi of Tsaphimi village, 14th Battalion, 5th Bde, Central Command, Naga Army. Abandoned in the jungle near Tarung river on 21st December, 1968.
17. Private Ghujukha Sumi of Mishilimi village 14th Battalion, 5th Brigade, Central Command, Naga Army. Killed in action at Tarung river on December 21, 1968.
18. Private Teisovilhou, son of Zakiecha of Kijümetouma village, 6th Battalion, 2nd Brigade, Southern Command, Naga Army. Killed in action at Tarung river on December 21, 1968.
19. Corporal Khiezeilie aka Azie, son of Putsolie Rutsa of Kohima village, 6th Battalion, 2nd Brigade, Southern Command, Naga Army. Succumbed to injury sustained at Tarung River on December 21, 1968
20. Private Mhiesilie Meru, son of Kruu Meru of Khonoma village, 4th Battalion, 2nd Brigade, Southern Command, Naga Army. Killed in action at Tarung River on December 21, 1968.
21. Private Thüleytsü Pochury of Phokhungri village, 10th Battalion, 4th Brigade, Central Command, Naga Army. Died of starvation in a forest in Burma, in December, 1968.
22. Private Viyiezo, son of Lhoukienyü of Jotsoma village, 4th Battalion, 2nd Brigade, Southern Command, Naga Army. Died of starvation in a forest in Burma on December 28, 1968.
23. Sergeant Major Luvishe Sumi of Surumi village, 4th Brigade Staff, Central command, Naga Army. Killed by Burmese Forces in a forest in Burma on December 30, 1968.

24. Private Tsoselie Seyie of Touphema village, 6th Battalion, 2nd Brigade, Southern Command, Naga Army. Died of starvation in a forest in Burma in December, 1968.
25. Private Tsoingki Samphury of Langturü village, 11th Battalion, Central Command, Naga Army. Killed in action at a jhum field at New Tikhao, on December 30, 1968.
26. Private Tsangkimung Samphury of Longkha village, 11th Battalion, Central Command, Naga Army. Killed in action at a jhum field at New Tikhao on December 30, 1968.
27. Private Zeneirpra Angami of Chiechema village, 6th Battalion, 2 Brigade, Southern Command, Naga Army. Killed in action at a jhum field at New Tikhao on 30th December, 1968.
28. Pte Yamukam Tikhir of Sangkhumti village, 4th Brigade staff, Central Command, Naga Army. Captured by Burmese Special Forces during 10 days starvation and executed at Tikhao village on the night of December 30, 1968.
29. Private Pfücha Angami of Kohima village, 6th Battalion, 2nd Brigade, Southern Command, Naga Army. Captured by Burmese Special Forces during 10 days starvation and executed at Tikhao village on the night of December 30, 1968.
30. Private Vitsomo Kense of Tuophema village, 6th Battalion, 2nd Brigade, Southern Command, Naga Army. Captured by Burmese Special Forces during 10 days starvation and executed at Tikhao village on the night of December 30, 1968.
31. Private Visizol Ltu aka Tehibu son of Sakhahe Ltu of Kidima village, 5th Battalion, 2nd Brigade, Southern Command, Naga Army. Killed in an ambush on January 3rd, 1969.
32. Corporal Pfülhuvi son of Seyieviko of Sechüma village, 4th Battalion, 2nd Brigade, Southern Command, Naga Army. Killed in an ambush on January 3rd, 1969.
33. Private Letuo Angami son of Neithou of Rüzhaphema village, 4th Battalion, 2nd Brigade, Southern Command, Naga Army. Killed in an ambush on January 3rd, 1969.
34. Corporal Yasie-o Rio of Tuophema village, 6th Battalion, 2nd Brigade, Southern Command, Naga Army. Succumbed to mine bomb injury on January 4th, 1969.
35. Corporal Yawhelie Angami of Phekerkriema village, 6th Battalion, 2nd Brigade, Southern Command, Naga Army. Died of mine bomb at Sanching forest.

36. Private Lhousakhonyu aka Bao, son of Pfüzavi of Jotsoma village, 4th Battalion, 2nd Brigade, Southern Command, Naga Army. Killed in action in a surprise attack at a village in Eastern Naga area, Burma.
37. Private Kenihosa Kintso son of Avül Kintso, of Kidima village, 5th Battalion, 2nd Brigade, Southern Command, Naga Army. Killed in action in a surprise attack at a village in Eastern Naga area, Burma.
38. Private Esol Khezho son of Viho Khezho of Khuzama village, 5th Battalion, 2nd Brigade, Southern Command, Naga Army. Killed in action in a surprise attack at a village in Eastern Naga area, Burma.
39. Sergeant Major Vitsolie aka Bvüu, son of Ziezolie of Jotsoma village, 4th Battalion, 2nd Brigade, Southern Command, Naga Army. Killed in an ambush at a Konyak village (Burma) on February 20, 1969.
40. Private Pusimo Kense of Tuophema village, 6th Battalion, 2nd Brigade, Southern Command, Naga Army. Succumbed to injury in an ambush at a Konyak village (Burma) on February 20, 1969.
41. Lieutenant Nyukhapa Pochury of Meluri village, 10th Battalion, 4th Brigade, Central Command, Naga Army. Killed in a fight at Lao village, on February 26, 1969.
42. Private Thinuoselhou, son of Yiechü of Rüsoma village, 6th Battalion, 2nd Brigade, Southern Command, Naga Army. Killed in a fight at Lao village, on February 26, 1969.
43. Private Khiungakiu Tikhir aka Khiunga of Sangkhumti village, 4th Brigade staff, Central Command, Naga Army. Killed in action at Tsonkhao outpost on February 28, 1969.
44. Corporal Suolahie Angami of Kohima village, 6th Battalion, 2nd Brigade, Southern Command, Naga Army. Killed in action in Eastern Naga area.
45. Private Pupa Lese of Mima village, 5th Battalion, 2nd Brigade, Southern Command, Naga Army. Killed by Village Guards (V.G) in Nagaland.
46. Lance Corporal Satoi Wotsa of Ghokimi village, 14th Battalion, 5th Bde, Central Command, Naga Army. Killed by Village Guards of Sangkhumti village in March, 1969.
47. Private Nzanpemo Lotha of Mekokla village, 17th Battalion, 6 Bde, Central command, Naga Army. Killed at a Khiamniungan village, by Village Guards.
48. Private Chiu Tikhir of Chiliso village, 4th Brigade staff, Central Command, Naga Army. Sacrificed his life defending Th. Muivah in Kachin Land.

Appendix III

Heroes Detained for Life in Indian Prisons

1. Mowu Angami, son of Jatsuvilie of village Khonoma
2. Lhouvicha, son of Pocha of village Puchama
3. Niethoselie Angami, son of Zhokru of village Zhakhama
4. Ahoto Sema, son of Heto of village Mishilimi
5. Gwovilie Angami, son of Dotseilie of village Nerhema
6. Ngusa Angami, son of Kucha of village Mima
7. Kezeihol Angami, son of Krocha of village Khuzama
8. Beilho Angami, son of Vover of village Chiechama
9. Kietuolie Angami, son of Kruvilie of village Kohima
10. Kahie Angami, son of Salhu of village Viphoma
11. Salie Angami, son of Puchelie of village Kohima
12. Vichanei Angami, son of Vidulhu of village Mima
13. Ketsohu Angami, son of Razukilie of village Mengouzuma
14. Lhoupralie Angami, son of Pulhousa of village Rukhoma
15. Nieruzhao Angami, son of Dengdevie of village Rezoma
16. Seikuolie Angami, son of Vilhoulie of village Kohima
17. Kushokha Sumi, son of Khaniti of village Ighanumi
18. Pukhato Sumi, son of Inashe of village Shesulimi
19. Heshena Sumi, son of Khupu of village Natsumi
20. Mesievi Angami, son of Muputuo of village Nerhema
21. Vizotuo Angami, son of Videlhulie of village Kohima
22. Lhousinyu Angami, son of Vihulie of village Nerhema
23. Krutsolie Angami, son of Neitsümo of village Tuophema
24. Khrielakuo Angami, son of Phoulie of village Kohima
25. Khiezo Angami son of Chou of village Kohima
26. Thepuselhou Angami, son of Nephi of village Mezoma
27. Mhiduo Angami, son of Kemehyu of village Vephoma

28. Khrietuo Angami, son of Mhesieu of village Chemima
29. Zuhie Angami, Sanguto Angami son Pekruvito of village Khonoma
30. Sanguto Angami, son Pekruvito of village Khonoma
31. Megosazo Angami, son of Nivese of village Khonoma
32. Sakole Angami, son of Vikocha of village Kigwema
33. Lhounizo Angami, son of Lhounu of village Rokhuma
34. Inavi Sumi, son of Kiviqhe of Mukalimi
35. Vikuokhoto Angami, son of Nilhuto of village Khonoma
36. Karutsu Pochury, son of Ralipong of village Sütsü
37. Nisa Angami, son of Dibu of village Sochunoma
38. Shutümi Pochury, son of Shoshemu of village Phor
39. Hekiye Sumi, son of Thungso of village Vedami
40. Laxheje Sumi, son of Khuhoto of village Shoixe
41. Qhuhoi Sumi, son of Hovukhu of village Tsutoho
42. Itokhu Sumi, son of Vikulho of village Luvishe
43. Kiyeto Sumi, son of Ghozuhe of village Surumi
44. Yekhalu Sumi, son of Khozuxe of village Lizumi
45. Luashemung Samphury, son of Thulachu of village Lalungru
46. Tsangkhuchu Samphury, son of Nokenchu of village Lantur
47. Engo Niangpa Konyak, son of Engo of village Ukha
48. Shikhu K. Sumi, son of Mukhuzu of village Sutimi
49. Khamkhui Tangkhul, son of Mayaothei of village Lampui (Ramva)
50. Samatai Tangkhul, son of Changpui of Ukhrul
51. Irengba Dharma Singh, son of Ibomcha Ngamthong, Manipuri
52. L.M. Shaniyi Mao, son of Mayu of village Tungjoy
53. Ngairem Phungshok Tangkhul, son of Chinaongai of village Somdol
54. Honrei Muivah Tangkhul, son of ShanozanofUkhrul
55. Khayapshai ShimrayTangkhul, son of Moreiphung of village Tuinem
56. Dr. Samson Luikham Tangkhul, son of N. Luikham of Ukhrul
57. Vibunuo Angami, son of Khrieru of village Pfechuma
58. Ruuzielie Angami son of Khenieze of village Keruma
59. Kheo Angami, son of Kuozielie of village Kohima
60. Lheo Angami, son of Mekrao of village Kohima
61. Lhoutsonyi Angami, son of Soliezu of village Kohima
62. Tsupichu Pochury, son of Sachu of village phor
63. Tsupitu Pochury, son of Tarachu of village phor
64. Pukhashe Sumi, son of Inakhu of village Hebolimi
65. Dikhu Angami, son of Pelhoupfu of village Kigwema
66. Tsonoho Angami, son of Vipiho of village Kesoma
67. Nichumelie Angami, son of Pfeto of village Khonoma

68. Punil Angami, son of Lhukhol of village Khuzama
69. Zelulie Angami, son of Pihutsu of village Phesama
70. Heshito Sumi, son of Akhalu of village Lazami
71. Khrienyupheu Angami, son of Thepfui of village Mazoma
72. Khoo Angami, son of Pelie of village Khonoma
73. Xukiye Sumi, son of Mulhe of village Iphonumi
74. Salumo Sumi, son of Lachekhu of village Mishilimi
75. Avito Sumi, son of Kigho of village Ighanumi
76. Kivito Sumi, son of Shikhu of village Natsumi
77. Kelhoulezo Angami, son of Doselie of village Rukhuma
78. Thenuovilie Angami, son of Divicha of village Keruma
79. Viyesielie Angami, son of Kruo of village Kohima
80. Peletsu Angami, son of Punazi of village Dihoma
81. Setou Angami, son of Luchalie of village Kigwema
82. Vow Angami, son of Tsutsawo of village Chiechama
83. Savil Angami, son of Douchol of village Viswema
84. Visielhou Angami, son of Gwokhrielie of village Dehoma
85. Chavi Angami, son of Pfyche of village Chiechama
86. Diethonyu Angami, son of Dukolie of village Keruma
87. Ruzukhrie, son of Lhousaru Kense of village Tophema
88. Nicho Angami, son of Putso of village Chakhabama
89. Vitolie Angami, son of Lhousime of village Tuophema
90. Tholhou Angami, son of Lhonie of village Kigwema
91. Chepong Pochuryson, son of Luchethi of village Sütsü
92. Nihozu Sumi, son of Izukhu of village Tsukomi
93. Ritatu Pochury, son of Ruchu of village Phor
94. Vihei Sumi, son of Vikhuto of village Qhekiye
95. Zuheto Sumi, son of Kokhuhe of village Lithsumi
96. Honivi Sumi, son of Chehoto of village Melahumi
97. Tokiye Sumi, son of Hashihe of village Achikuchumi
98. Inuvi Sumi, son of Hokhupu of village Surumi
99. Nchupomo Lotha, son of Rothungo of village Changsu Old.
100. Ghohuto Sumi, son of Jehoto of village Jekiye
101. Zuhei Sumi, son of Phuhokhu of village Thakiye
102. Mlayi Samphury, Son of Tsangtichu of village Lantur
103. Thongtsi Tikhir, son of Ahuse of village Chikipongru
104. Longpungchu Samphury, son of Matru of village Lantur
105. Ghohevi Sumi, son of Luheto of village Sutimi
106. Zuheto Sumi, son of Phuhoxu of village Lukhami
107. Kishotshu Sangtam, son of Tsaiki of village Natsami

Appendix III 219

108. RisumongTikhir, son of Yongpenthong of village Thonoknyu
109. Nitsuhu Angami, son of Vilhuru of village Chiechama
110. Piwoto Sumi, son of Shihani of village Ighanumi
111. Jehoto Sumi, son of Kupuzu of village Lukhami

General Dusoi and 19 others (From Agra jail, Uttar Pradesh)

112. Dusoi Chakhesang, son of Motosi of village Yoruba
113. Povotso Chakhesang, son of Thingoi of village Ketsapome
114. Pulkhruvi, alias Puleksnyi, son of Chiseye of village Thevopisoma
115. Khruhucho Chakhesang, son of Vamohu of village Phasechadima
116. Vezhenyi, son of Kekhwuthi of village Yoruba
117. Shenuyi, alias Senuyi, son of Methanu of villaheKhuzami
118. Poleo Chakhesang, son of Vebuyi of village Thepfuzuma
119. Zachive Chakhesang, son of Verudu of village Phugwimi
120. Zeseru Chakhesang, son of Methalhu of village Yarubami
121. Kedulhunyi Chakhesang, son of Mezalo of village Zapami
122. Tochimong Yimchungru, son of Showuba of village Sangphur
123. Ramchi Yimchungru, son of Mukhe of village Kutowur
124. Hamphuba Yimchungru, son of Yansomong of village Pungro
125. Ngutsonyu Chakhesang, son of Pfukhrunyu of village Leshemi (Near Khezakonoma)
126. Mathanu Chakhesang, son of Pushoi of village Zulhami
127. Aheiwetso Chakhesang, son of Ditsoru of village Chizami
128. Chekhosui Chakhesang, son of Huchonyi of village Kikruma
129. Vetsucho Chakhesang, son of Tarunyo of village Kikruma
130. Chupelo Chakhesang, son of Lonyichu of village Yoseba
131. Valengoi Chakhesang, son of Lupohu of village Pfesachoduma

Three East Pakistanis

132. Mr Bashid Ahmed, son of Mohamad Usan of village Chaphaudiya, East Pakistan, (Present day Bangladesh)
133. Mr. Siddique, son of Bashir Ahmed of village Surburng, East Pakistan, (Present day Bangladesh)
134. Mr. Munir Ahmed, son of Amin Sharief of village Surburng, East Pakistan (Present day Bangladesh)

NB: Produced as recorded in the original copy of the charge sheet.

Appendix IV   **TRUE COPY OF DETENTION ORDER**

True Copy

Ground for detention of ...., Resident of village...............

In pursuance of Act, 1950 (4 of 1950), you ...., of village, District..............

That the grounds on which the order of 31st March, 1969, have been made are as under:

That:

(i) You are a member of the underground Naga hostiles who had obtained illegal arms and ammunitions and other assistance from foreign countries including China with the object of endangering the security of the State and maintenance of of public order.

(ii) In furtherance of this object, you crossed the border illegally without a proper passport and obtained arms and ammunitions and other assistance from foreign countries and re-entered India illegally with a view to endangering the security of State and the maintenance of public order.

(iii) In pursuance of your general design to commit acts of violence endangering the security of the State and maintenance of public order, you have been moving with dangerous lethal and unlicensed weapons and some of these weapons have been recovered from you.

(iv) You are being detained to prevent you from taking any further action in pursuance of your criminal design.

2. You are further informed that you have a right to make representation in writing against the order under which you are detained. If you wish to make such a representation, you should write to the Government of India through the Superintendent of Central Jail, Hazaribagh as soon as possible to the Advisory Board within 30 days of your detention and your representation, after which the case would not be considered by the Board.

3. You have the right of personal appearance before the Advisory Board for representing yourself. If you wish to do so, you have to inform the Government of India through the Superintendent, Hazaribagh Central Jail, Hazaribagh.

BY ORDER
AND IN THE NAME OF THE PRESIDENT
Sd/ 4.4.69
(G.S. KAPOOR)
UNDER SECRETARY TO THE GOVERNMENT OF INDIA

Copy, in duplicate, forwarded to the Superintendent, Hazaribagh Central Jail, Hazaribagh, for communicating and explaining the contents to the detenu and to give them one copy, not later than the 6th of April, 1969 and return other with endorsement of service.

Sd/ 4.4.69
(G.S. KAPOOR)
UNDER SECRETARY TO THE GOVERNMENT OF INDIA

Contact the Author by emailing
nagapekingjimo@gmail.com

INSPIRED TO WRITE A BOOK?

Contact
Maurice Wylie Media

Your Inspirational Christian Publisher

Based in Northern Ireland with a branch in Nagaland, distributing around the world.

www.MauriceWylieMedia.com